VARIETIES OF PRAYER

VARIETIES OF PRAYER

A Survey Report

MARGARET M. POLOMA
and
GEORGE H. GALLUP, JR.

TRINITY PRESS INTERNATIONAL   Philadelphia

First Published 1991

Second Printing 1992

Trinity Press International
3725 Chestnut Street
Philadelphia, PA 19104

Interior design and production: Publishers' WorkGroup
Cover design: Brian Preuss

Library of Congress Cataloging-in-Publication Data

Poloma, Margaret M.
    Varieties of prayer : a survey report / Margaret M. Poloma, George
H. Gallup
      p.   cm.
    Includes bibliographical references and index.
    ISBN 1-56338-008-0 (hard). — ISBN 1-56338-007-2 (pbk.)
    1. Prayer—United States.   2. United States—Religion—1960–
I. Gallup, George, 1930– . II. Title.
BL560.P65 1991
242--dc20   90-28578
                                                               CIP

Printed in the United States of America

To
LAURA M. HARRISON

CONTENTS

Acknowledgments ix

Foreword by David J. Hassel, S.J. xiii

1 What the Social Scientists Are Saying 1

2 What Do People Do When They Pray? 19
  Types of Prayer

3 Does God Really Speak? 43
  Religious Experiences during Prayer

4 Do Prayer and Politics Mix? 67
  Personal Prayer and Political Activism

5 Unless You Forgive Others 85
  Prayer and Forgiveness

6 To Comfort or to Challenge 107
  Prayer and Approaches to Religion

CONTENTS

7 Prayer and Community   125
   A Challenge to Churches

Methodology Appendix   137
   Design of the Samples

Index   139

ACKNOWLEDGMENTS

Research projects are born very often out of personal interest in a given topic. This one is no exception. We are among the nearly 90 percent of the American public that does pray. Furthermore, we are among the 60 percent that finds prayer to be a very important facet of their daily lives. Although aware of our respective personal prayer styles and aware of changes in them over time, we had only limited knowledge about what others did when they prayed and about the effects of prayer on their lives. We are grateful to those persons who participated in the 1988 Gallup Poll and in the 1985 Akron Area Survey which pretested the prayer questions, as well as to those who participated in qualitative interviews that enhanced our understanding of the survey findings. It was the survey participants and interviewees who made it possible to write *Varieties of Prayer: A Survey Report*.

Margaret Poloma's interest in researching prayer began in early 1985 as she prepared part of the instrument for that year's Akron Area Survey. She wishes to acknowledge the assistance given by McKee McClendon in constructing the instrument, in pretesting the items, and in serving as principal investigator for the Akron Area Survey from 1982 to 1988. The Akron Area Survey proved to be fertile ground for testing some hypotheses on the significance of prayer, results of which served as a basis for questions included in the 1988 Gallup Poll on religiosity in American life. A number of graduate students at the University of Akron were involved in data analysis for both projects. We wish to give recognition to James Quane, Jeffrey Breese, and Kirk Davis for their extensive work with the data. George Gallup's interest in the topic of forgiveness and its relationship to prayer owes much to Sister Miriam Murphy, S.N.D, Ph.D. This proved to be an especially fruitful area of investigation.

The special 1988 Gallup Survey on religion in American life from which our findings are derived was the product of cooperation among three organizations: the Society for the Scientific Study of Religion, the Religious Research Association, and the Gallup Organization. A special thank you to others who represented these groups, especially Richard Gorsuch, Sarah Jones, Jill Kiekolt, Kirk Hadaway, and Wade Clark Roof.

We are unable to acknowledge the many persons who read sections of this manuscript or heard the presentation of preliminary reports and then offered helpful comments. Their support was a source of encouragement during the many months of data analysis and writing up the results. We especially benefitted from the careful reading and critique of the entire manuscript by David J. Hassel, S.J. Father Hassel's expertise as a spiritual director has given him insight into various prayer forms that is not easily accessible to social scientists. His assurance that our survey did capture the diversity of prayer forms and his confidence in our work was a great encouragement to us.

Finally, we wish to acknowledge the help of Harold W. Rast, Th.D., director of Trinity Press International. The enthusiasm he has shown for our work instilled a fresh spirit as we revised our final draft of this manuscript.

Our work answered many questions we personally had on prayer, while raising still others to be answered in future research. We hope that our findings, clearly demonstrating the importance of prayer in the lives of Americans, will generate more scientific investigation. More importantly we hope that *Varieties of Prayer* will be useful in setting up programs to teach people the art of how to pray effectively. Based on our analysis of survey data, we can state without reservation that the single most important characteristic of effective prayer is the ability to commune with God. Prayer needs to go beyond ritual, opening the door to a relationship with the One for whom the human heart has been made. Our prayer is that the fruits of our research may in some small way facilitate the opening of that door.

George Gallup, Jr.
Margaret M. Poloma

FOREWORD

There are some interesting surprises contained in Dr. Margaret Poloma's sociological study, *Varieties of Prayer*. One of the surprises is that between 1872 and 1985 only sixteen sociologists attempted to isolate empirically the phenomena of prayer and to analyze them—despite the fact that prayer is so prevalent and so powerful in people's lives, especially in times of stress. One of the deterrents to such research probably has been the difficulty of getting so-called hard data. But with some remarkably astute experiential-type questions, Dr. Poloma and Dr. Gallup (in the latter's 1988 poll on religion in American life) have managed to secure definite factual responses. (I found only one question ambiguous; of course, it yielded no correlation.)

Further surprises occur in the conclusions drawn from the data. For example, the number of people praying (88%) is larger than I had expected. It may well be that I have underestimated the hunger people have for some contact with God amid all the "easy living" of which American culture is often accused. A second example: Dr. Poloma has managed to discover the large number of people gifted with more passive or

meditative prayer (42% of those praying), a sign of mature spiritual living even though the Princeton Religious Research
Report declares that American prayer life is "underdeveloped
and undernourished." A last example: a solid correlation is
found between strong prayer life and political activism on both
a local and national level.

We have long admired the thoroughness of the Gallup
polls so that we are not surprised to find that every section of
the United States and every stratum of its society is pinpointed.
In this way it is not hard to compare societal strata, national sections, demographic data (age, sex, education, marital status,
income), and various denominations. This alone makes
Varieties of Prayer useful not only to the sociologist but also to
theologians, pastoral directors, and counselors. These latter will
appreciate especially the real-life stories illustrating conclusions
and the earthy phenomena used to describe the varieties of
prayer and to determine grades of God-consciousness within
prayer experience. A brief glance at Dr. Gallup's Chapter 7, in
which the authors further sharpen and sum up the conclusions
of the book, will convince the browser that this is a book worth
reading in its totality.

The table of contents demonstrates the logical organization of the book as well as its content. But it cannot reveal the
authors' careful, statistical factor-analysis employed with bivariate correlations, nor show the stringent procedure of multiple
regression used to check these correlations so that the validity
of conclusions may be fixed more securely.

A debt of gratitude is owed to Dr. Poloma and to Dr.
Gallup for the many months of work involved in gathering all
the data and in interpreting it not only for the specialist but also
for the ordinary reader. Indeed, the specialist in sociology of
religion will recognize a new area for research opening up,
while the ordinary reader will find the data, comparisons, and

conclusions of this study a challenge for prayer life and an insight into the socio-demography of those seeking guidance in prayer.

David J. Hassel, S.J.
Loyola University of Chicago

1

WHAT THE
SOCIAL SCIENTISTS
ARE SAYING

> We hear, in these days of scientific enlightenment, a great deal
> of discussion about the efficacy of prayer; and many reasons are
> given us why we should not pray, whilst others are given us why
> we should. But in all this very little is said of the reason why we
> *do* pray, which is simply that we cannot *help* praying. It seems
> probable that, in spite of all that "science" may do to the con-
> trary, men will continue to pray to the end of time, unless their
> mental nature changes in a manner which nothing we know
> should lead us to expect. The impulse to pray is a necessary
> consequence of the fact that whilst the innermost of the empiri-
> cal selves of man is a Self of the *social* sort, it yet can find its only
> adequate *Socius* in an ideal world.
>
> William James
> *Psychology*, x

An overwhelming number of Americans claim to engage
in prayer. Gallup Reports for over four decades show little
change in the percentage of persons who respond affirmatively
to the question, "Do you ever pray?" Ninety percent of those
surveyed in 1948 said they prayed; thirty years later, 89 percent
acknowledged that they prayed to God. In 1988, the year the

1

survey was conducted for *Varieties of Prayer*, 88 percent of the respondents polled acknowledged that they engaged in prayer.

Despite these well-known and undisputed figures, social scientists have shown little interest in the topic. William James, a pioneer in social psychology whose interest in religious experience included discussions of prayer, shared with other founding fathers a deep interest in the study of religion that is not found among most contemporary scholars. As sociologist William Swatos has noted, any number of reasons may be advanced for this indifference of researchers, particularly toward the study of prayer. One of the assumptions made is that prayer is an "irrational act" and not worthy of serious study by social scientists. In other words, the positivistic origins of sociology, psychology, and other behavioral sciences have created a bias against granting any credence to the practice. Swatos (1987:103) concludes, "People pray, and that is all a sociologist needs to know to begin work."

Such occasional calls for research on prayer fall largely on deaf ears. This dearth of empirical research is reflected in social science texts on religion. Leading books make either no mention of prayer or limit themselves to the controversial issue of prayer in the schools. The authors of one psychology text (which atypically did give a portion of a chapter to prayer) noted that the existing findings are inconclusive and contradictory. They concluded that attempts to study prayer may be futile:

> If a deity can meaningfully answer a believer's prayer, and if prayer is to remain a spiritual rather than a magical exercise, then surely that same deity would make sure that all empirical studies of the efficacy of prayer will turn out inconclusive! The evidence for the effectiveness of prayers, as they touch events in the material world remains outside the domain of science. The faithful who want to believe can believe, and the skeptic who chooses not to believe could not be convinced. (Meadow and Kahoe, 1984:120)

This kind of logic has never stopped social scientists from wrestling with other subjects that are difficult to measure and on which research findings are inconclusive. It is more likely that social scientists, many of whom are personally indifferent or skeptical about prayer, simply have no interest in investing time and energy into its study. Much of what we do know about prayer in American life comes to us through the descriptive information provided by the Gallup opinion polls.

GALLUP REPORTS ON PRAYER

Although the percentage of persons who report that they, at least on occasion, do pray has been relatively constant for over four decades, there has been a decrease in the frequency of prayer. For example, the proportion of Americans who pray, on the average, twice a day or more declined from 42 percent in 1952 to 27 percent in 1978. Since then, however, the number of those praying twice or more daily has shown a slight increase to 31 percent. One of the contributing factors in this decrease in the frequency of prayer may be related to a parallel decline in the percentage of Americans who say grace out loud before family meals. This figure has decreased from 69 percent in 1962 to 57 percent in 1979. The Gallup Reports indicate surprisingly little difference among population groups in the proportion who ever pray. Some differences emerge, however, among those who pray three times a day or more. While the overall national figure for this group is 19 percent, the percentages for women (23%), older persons (24%), blacks (23%), and Protestants (22%) are significantly higher than for comparison groups in each category.

Gallup and Jones (1989:36) report that 88 percent of Americans pray to God, while 76 percent agree that prayer is "an important part" of their daily lives—"findings that suggest the enormous extent of private piety in the U.S., which coexists with notable expressions of self-reliance." This emphasis on self-reliance is reflected in the Gallup finding that 45 percent of the respondents of one survey claimed to rely more on themselves than on a higher power to solve life's problems. In contrast, a smaller yet significant minority of 36 percent reported relying more on a "higher power, such as God," in solving the problems of life, with an additional 17 percent volunteering the response that they rely on both self and God (Gallup and Jones, 1989:46). While the largest single group of respondents seemed to reflect a belief in the maxim "God helps those who help themselves," a significant minority reported being most likely to rely on God. If this minority is combined with those who volunteered the response of relying both on self and on God, the majority of Americans appear to regard God's help as important in dealing with life's problems.

This mix of self-reliance and reliance on God may be illustrated through yet another finding from a Gallup survey. Respondents were asked, "When you are faced with a problem or crisis, to which of the following kinds of support would you likely turn for help?" Respondents were instructed to select as many of the following choices as applied: share it (the problem) with family, share it with close friends, discuss it with a class or group in your church or synagogue, work it through on your own, read the Bible or other inspirational literature, seek help from a religious counselor, seek other professional counseling, seek help from a support group, pray about it. The most common answer indicated the family as a source of support (87%), but working through problems on their own (80%) and prayer (80%) were tied as the second most common response (Gallup and Jones, 1989:62). Judging from these responses, it appears that prayer is important to the vast majority of Americans, particularly during times of crisis, although it may be coupled with strong feelings of self-reliance as well as support from family and friends.

The importance of prayer for Americans receives additional documentation from yet another Gallup poll query: "Please tell me how much you agree or disagree with this statement: 'Prayer is an important part of my life.'" Forty-one percent of a national sample completely agreed with the statement, with another 35 percent "mostly" agreeing. Only 23 percent either "mostly" or "completely" disagreed. Gallup and Jones (1989:38–39), however, noted some important differences among the respondents:

> Most apt to cite the importance of daily prayer are women (82%), non-whites (90%), those without a high school degree (84%), persons over 50 (85%), and Evangelicals or self-described born-again Christians (93%). Groups less inclined to stress daily prayer are men (69%), college graduates (65%), persons under 30 (68%), and Jews (36%). Catholics and Protestants at 80% each say that prayer is an important daily exercise.

The Gallup reports suggest that one of the reasons prayer may be so important to the majority of Americans is due to perceptions of its efficacy in improving a sense of well-being. When asked how prayer affects their thoughts or actions, people's most common responses were "It makes me feel good" and "It gives me peace of mind." The results of another Gallup survey showed a large majority of respondents (94%) reporting "prayer, meditation, or reading the Bible" as being very effective in dealing with discouragement or depression. Paradoxically, however, despite such a positive attribution to spiritual remedies, a much smaller percent (48%) reported using prayer, meditation, or Bible reading to fight their own struggles against discouragement or depression (Gallup and Jones, 1989:64–65).

After reviewing these and other Gallup findings, a special issue on prayer in American life (*Emerging Trends* [1985:4], a publication of the Princeton Religious Research Center) concluded:

If one is a religionist, one cannot help but be impressed by the survey finding that as many as nine in ten Americans continue to seek a power outside themselves for guidance for their lives.

It also should be noted that for most Americans, prayer is important in their lives. They believe in the power of prayer and believe their prayers are answered.

Furthermore, Americans want their faith to grow and at least one in five (19%) feels the churches could better serve them by helping them deepen their prayer lives.

While these findings may be encouraging, it should also be noted that surveys give clear evidence that our prayer life appears to be underdeveloped and undernourished.

Such informative descriptive data should have generated inferential studies by social scientists to learn more about the process, types of, and effects of prayer. On the contrary, many, perhaps most social scientists are unaware of such statistics. Theoretical writings from a social science perspective have been few and far between while research has been nearly nonexistent. From the meager literature that does exist, two preliminary issues will be explored briefly from the social science literature: What is prayer? and Does prayer make a difference?

SOCIAL SCIENTISTS ON PRAYER

William James, in his classic book, *The Varieties of Religious Experience*, defined prayer as "every kind of inward communion or conversation with the power recognized as divine." Other scholars have suggested that this communion takes primarily two forms: verbal prayer and meditative prayer. Verbal prayer has commonly been subdivided into such categories as thanksgiving, petition, intercession, and adoration. Meditative prayer tends to be less active than verbal prayer, with the person relating to God in a passive, undemanding, open, and nonverbal way. The empirical studies that have been done on prayer have attempted to explore the types of prayer and prayer's impact on the lives of those who pray. A review of these studies through 1985 had been conducted by psychologists John R. Finney and H. Newton Malony. Their findings are worth summarizing here.

Reviewing the Empirical Studies

In their extensive review of empirical studies on Christian prayer, Finney and Malony reported that only sixteen studies could be found for the period 1872 through the mid-1980s. These were studies that focused on prayer and did not include research that may have included Gallup-like questions to determine the frequency of prayer activities but did not seek to determine the possible effects of prayer. Neither did the review include studies of glossolalia, or "praying in tongues," which although practiced by only one or two percent of the population has captured the attention of scores of researchers. Included were those studies that sought to explore the nature of and process of prayer as well as those which sought to determine whether prayer made a difference in the pray-er's life.

In reviewing these studies, Finney and Malony divided them into four groups: (1) developmental studies of conceptions of prayer; (2) research on the motivations for praying; (3) studies of the effects of verbal prayer; and (4) studies of the effects of meditative prayer. The findings of each of these subtopics merit some brief attention.

Developmental Studies on
Conceptions of Prayer

Six psychological studies were found that dealt with the development of prayer among children and adolescents. With increasing age, it appears there is less of a belief that prayer will have material consequences. And as a child matures chronologically there is a change in the content of prayer from egocentric petitions for such things as candy and toys to altruistic desires for such things as peace on earth. A third conclusion of the research on the development of prayer in childhood is that a child's concept of prayer develops from vague associations with the term "God" to a private conversation with God in which intimate things are shared. In other words, the evidence suggests that changes in prayer coincide with stages in a child's development, with adolescents praying more altruistically and intimately than younger children.

Motivations for Praying

Finney and Malony identified only one study which empirically explored the motives for prayer. In 1947, A.T. Welford raised the question, "Is religious behavior dependent upon affect or frustration?" After analyzing information collected from sixty-three male students, Welford (1947) concluded, "Any simple hypothesis which regards prayer as a response merely to distressing, threatening forces in the environment is inadequate." Prayers of petition appear to be motivated both by the need to reduce frustration and the need to adjust to unusual situations. Such prayers can also be a positive means of adjustment to difficulties of life. It would appear that this topic could be fertile ground for psychological research. To date, however, researchers have found it of little interest.

Effects of Verbal Prayer

One of the earliest studies on prayer was undertaken by Francis Galton and written up in an article published in 1872. Galton studied the average life expectancies of various affluent English groups and found that members of the royal houses had the lowest average life expectancy. This was found to be the case despite the tradition of praying for royalty. He concluded that there is no statistical evidence for the objective value of petitionary prayer since these prayers had no measurable effect on the longevity of those prayed for. Although Galton's study and reasoning would be faulted by modern social scientists, his study is noteworthy. He had the courage to do a pioneering study of a central religious practice that continues to be neglected.

More than eighty years later another major study was published on the effects of verbal prayer. In 1957 William Parker's experiment was reported in a nontechnical book co-authored with Elaine St. Johns and titled *Prayer Can Change Your Life*. As Finney and Malony summarize Parker's experiment:

> Parker's subjects were forty-five volunteers ranging in age from 22 to 60. They were all suffering from either psychosomatic symptoms or experiencing considerable subjective emotional distress. The subjects were assigned to one of three groups, each containing fifteen persons. Group I received weekly individual psychotherapy sessions. The people in this group expressed either a preference for psychotherapy or had been advised by their physicians to seek this treatment. Group 2 was labeled the "Random Pray-ers." The subjects in this group were practicing Christians who agreed to pray daily that their specific problems would be overcome. They prayed in their accustomed manner. Group 3 was the Prayer Therapy group which followed a specified program for religious growth. (Finney and Malony, 1985:111)

Using a battery of psychological tests during this nine-month experiment, Parker reported an average of 72 percent improvement for the Prayer Therapy group and a 65 percent improvement for those involved in weekly individual psychotherapy sessions. The Random Pray-ers showed no improvement. Although this study has a number of weaknesses, its results do encourage further investigation of programs that used petitionary prayer as a therapeutic technique. Parker's design and reporting of data make it impossible to sort out the effects of verbal prayer from other components of the Prayer Therapy group. Limited research conducted on the topic after Parker's pioneering efforts seems to suggest that verbal prayer alone is not effective in reducing anxiety.

The Effects of
Contemplative Prayer

Only two studies of contemplative prayer have been carried out, both on select samples of Catholics. In 1977 Marilyn Mallory published her work on members of the Discalced Carmelite Order, and in 1979 Howard Sacks reported on his study of the effect of the Ignatian Spiritual Exercises on fifty male subjects. Given the special target study groups, it is difficult to generalize the findings to wider populations. Finney and Malony do suggest that from Sacks it can be inferred that perhaps contemplative prayer may facilitate integration of the self-system.

Two other recent studies conducted by medical researchers and not included in the Finney and Malony review also deserve some attention. One series of investigations conducted by Harvard cardiologist Herbert Benson investigated the medical benefits of personal meditation on general health. Another cardiologist, Randolf Byrd of San Francisco General Hospital, used an experimental design to explore the effects of intercessory prayer on the recovery of coronary patients. Although both are examples of medical research, the results complement the findings of social scientists on prayer and should be briefly discussed.

Medical Science Explores the
Benefits of Prayer

Herbert Benson's journey toward the study of prayer began in 1968 when he started researching the physical effects of meditation. At that time he limited himself to researching persons who were practicing Transcendental Meditation or TM as taught by followers of Maharishi Mahesh Yogi. Meditation was found to lower metabolic rates, slow heart rates, lower blood pressure, and slow breathing. Benson published his findings in a 1975 best-selling book, *The Relaxation Response.*

Benson became convinced of the benefits of the particular kind of meditation produced by the recitation of a mantra. In fact, the relaxation response could be produced through the use of any word, not only the mantra used by those who practiced TM. Despite the physical benefits of using meaningless words in meditation, there was some difficulty in keeping people involved in the program. The villain was boredom. Many persons quit meditating despite the fact that the relaxation response brought significant benefits, reducing headaches, hypertension, and other ailments. It was at this point that Benson began to study persons who prayed, finding that they were less likely to succumb to boredom and were more likely to stick with the program (Kiesling and Harris, 1989).

Benson introduced the notion of the *faith factor*, suggesting that the benefits of faith may interact with the direct physiological benefits of the relaxation response. He summarized his conclusions based on years of research as follows:

> My study in this field has convinced me that, for whatever reason, faith does make a difference in enhancing the power of the mind over health and disease. In other words, the Faith Factor—or combination of the Relaxation Response with a profound set of personal convictions—can provide at least two benefits not available through ordinary relaxation or meditative techniques: (1) it can encourage a person to be more persistent in following a regular Relaxation-Response program; and (2) it can combine the beneficial effects of the Relaxation Response with those of the placebo effect. (Benson, 1984:146)

While Benson's study explored the power of the mind over the body, Randolf Byrd's research took a somewhat different tack. Byrd explored the effects of prayers of intercessors on the recovery of coronary patients who did not know they were being prayed for. Using a sample of 393 coronary care unit patients at San Francisco General Hospital, Byrd had "born again" Christians who prayed daily and were active in their local churches serve as intercessors for a random group of patients. (Intercessors were not assigned to a random control group, a group that later proved to be like the experimental group in all ways except that of being assigned pray-ers.) Each patient, unknown to him or her, was given three to seven intercessors who prayed daily "for a rapid recovery and for the prevention of complications and death." Byrd (1988:827) states, "I collected the information on each patient in a blinded manner, without knowledge of the spiritual status, condition, or ideas of the entrants during the study."

Byrd's intent in conducting this experimental study of prayer and patients in a general hospital coronary care unit was designed to answer a basic question: Does intercessory prayer to the Judeo-Christian God have any effect on the patient's medical condition and recovery while in the hospital? The answer in this well-designed study appears to be Yes. Byrd (1988:829) reports:

> Analysis of events after entry into the study showed the prayer group had less congestive heart failure, required less diuretic and antibiotic therapy, had fewer episodes of pneumonia, had fewer cardiac arrests, and were less frequently intubated and ventilated.

In other words, Byrd's findings suggest that intercessory prayer, even when such prayer is not known to the person who is the object of the intercession, appears to be therapeutically beneficial.

ANOTHER EMPIRICAL LOOK
AT PRAYER

The research findings that do exist strongly suggest that prayer deserves further study. With the exception of Gallup's statistics, most studies were conducted on very select groups of persons: a small sample of students, patients in therapy, women in cloistered religious life, and subjects of medical research. One can infer from the results of these limited studies, however, that prayer can make a difference in the lives of all people.

On the other hand, the information coming from studies that represent a larger population (such as that reported by Gallup) has been limited largely to description (as opposed to making inferences about the nature and effects of prayer). Recognizing the paucity of data on prayer and the limitations of existing inferential studies, Margaret Poloma did a preliminary local survey in Akron, Ohio, in 1985 which served as base from which to launch the more extensive national survey conducted by the Gallup Organization in the fall of 1988. Some of these findings will be reviewed to illustrate how prayer may be making a difference in the lives of everyday Americans.

Poloma assumed the position of faculty investigator for the 1985 survey conducted annually by the sociology department of the University of Akron with the intention of doing an extensive analysis of the different facets of religiosity. After reviewing the existing studies on prayer, she felt that this topic deserved particular attention. The telephone survey netted 575 respondents believed to be representative of the Akron, Ohio, area. Analysis of these data suggested that prayer did indeed make a difference.

The focus of the Akron Area Survey has been on general well-being. Each year questions are asked about how satisfied Akronites are with such things as their health, marital status, and standard of living, as well as questions that measure a general level of satisfaction and happiness. In 1985 Poloma wanted to see whether religious factors led to an increase in feelings of well-being. As she had hypothesized, religion was found to be an important contributor to perceptions of well-being. She not only found her hypotheses to hold, but she also found that prayer measures often demonstrated stronger relationships with well-being than other commonly used religiosity items. In other words, more frequently used indicators of religiosity, including church membership and religious beliefs, tended to show weaker relationships with well-being than did some prayer measures.[1]

In a more detailed data-analysis done with Brian Pendleton, it was found that the frequency of prayer was not particularly relevant to well-being measures (Poloma and Pendleton, 1989; 1991). In fact the evidence was that when other controls were introduced, people who prayed more frequently but did not have religious experiences were *more* likely to be dissatisfied with their lives than those who prayed less often. It is not that prayer *causes* dissatisfaction with life; it is more likely that problems and crises cause people who ordinarily pray only infrequently to increase their times of prayer. Being relatively unskilled in prayer, they may not know how to experience the comfort that others have enjoyed through encountering God. Their prayers do not seem to change their situations nor do they offer comfort; in fact they appear to exacerbate dissatisfaction with the way their lives are going. In short, such people may be using prayer as a kind of last resort. Their dissatisfaction seems to increase as their problems remain unresolved, and they are

---

1. For example, the correlation between religious belief and reported satisfaction with life was .13, while the correlation between experiences of God during prayer and life satisfaction was .20. Similarly the relationship between church membership and satisfaction with one's religious life was .26, while the correlation between prayer experiences and religious satisfaction was .50.

left without the comfort that comes from an encounter with the divine.

Far more important to well-being scores was (1) whether or not respondents had religious experiences during prayer, and (2) what they did when they prayed. The experience of God during prayer—feeling his presence, being led by him, finding that specific prayer requests were answered—was more important in contributing to subjective perceptions of well-being (i.e., life satisfaction, feeling that life had a meaning and purpose, reporting a sense of general happiness, and religious satisfaction) than was the frequency with which a person invoked God. These prayer experiences were related to four kinds of activities in prayer: meditative, conversational, petitionary, and ritual. In terms of the two major types of prayer discussed earlier— verbal and meditative—these four types could be reclassified as meditative and three distinctive types of verbal (conversational, petitionary, and ritual). Our findings suggest that meditative pray-ers (who are less active and more passive in their communion with God) are most likely to have intense experiences of God during prayer. Those who rely on ritual prayer are the least likely to report prayer experiences.[2] Of the types of prayer explored, meditative prayer seems to have the strongest relation to the measures of well-being. In other words, not all forms of prayer are equally likely to affect a person's perceptions of well-being. Those who rely on petitionary prayer and ritualistic prayer forms are not as likely to be satisfied with their lives as those who employ meditative or conversational prayer.

These findings on prayer seemed significant. It was at this

---

2. The strongest correlation between experiences of God during prayer, a scale that will be discussed in detail in the next chapter, and a particular prayer type exists with meditative prayer ($r = .70$). The correlations between the other prayer forms and prayer experiences are as follows: conversational prayer, $r = .57$; petitionary prayer, $r = .41$; and ritual prayer, $r = .17$.

point, while working with George Gallup, Jr., on an extensive national religiosity survey co-sponsored by the Religious Research Association and the Society for the Scientific Study of Religion, that Poloma asked whether a number of questions on prayer activities and prayer experiences could be included. Questions on prayer were asked in this Gallup survey that had not been measured before in a general population of Americans. This survey, conducted in the fall of 1988, provides the data for *Varieties of Prayer*. The results permit us to deal with questions on prayer that have not been discussed previously by social scientific research—questions such as What do people do when they pray? and Do people feel they really hear from God? These prayer activities and prayer experiences will be related to demographic factors, including age, sex, income, and denominational differences. Finally, and perhaps most importantly, some effects of prayer will be explored—on political activism, on the ability to forgive injuries, on perceptions of what makes a good Christian or a good Jew, and on life satisfaction.

We have long known that Americans pray. If social psychologist William James was correct in his observation, men and women will always pray. The statistics presented in these pages suggest that prayer is a more widely practiced activity than sex, yet far more is known about the sexual practices of Americans than about their prayer lives! It is time to lift the unspoken taboo that has operated in the social sciences and that has led to the benign neglect of this near universal activity. Using the data generated by interviews with 1,030 respondents representing all regions of the United States, this book will raise and answer some questions about prayer that have not been researched before.

The next chapter will consider the question, What do people do when they pray? In it we will explore the four major types of prayer and how these different types of prayer may be seen to reflect perceptions of intimacy with God.

WORKS CITED

Benson, Herbert
  1975   *The Relaxation Response.* New York: William Morrow.
  1984   *Beyond the Relaxation Response.* New York: Times Books.
Byrd, Randolf C.
  1988   Positive Therapeutic Effects of Intercessory Prayer in a Coronary Care Unit Population. *Southern Medical Journal* 81 (7) (July):826–29.
Finney, John R., and H. Newton Malony, Jr.
  1985   Empirical Studies of Christian Prayer: A Review of the Literature. *Journal of Psychology and Theology* 4 (2):104–15.
Gallup Report
  1985   *Religion in America. 50 Years: 1935–1985.* Report no. 236 (May). Princeton, N.J.
Gallup, George, Jr., and Sarah Jones
  1989   *One Hundred Questions and Answers: Religion in America.* Princeton, N.J.: Princeton Research Center.
James, William
  1963   *The Varieties of Religious Experience.* New York: University Books. Originally published 1902.
Kiesling, Stephen, and T. George Harris
  1989   The Prayer War. *Psychology Today* (October):65–66.
Mallory, Marilyn May
  1977   *Christian Mysticism: Transcending Techniques.* Amsterdam: Van Gorcum Assoc.
Meadow, Mary Jo, and Richard D. Kahoe
  1984   *Psychology of Religion.* New York: Harper & Row.
Parker, William R., and Elaine St. Johns
  1957   *Prayer Can Change Your Life.* Carmel, N.Y.: Guideposts.
Poloma, Margaret M., and Brian F. Pendleton
  1989   Exploring Types of Prayer and the Quality of Life. *Review of Religious Research* 31 (September):46–53.
  1991   The Effects of Prayer and Prayer Experiences on Measures of Well-Being. *Journal of Psychology and Theology* 19(1):71–83.
Princeton Religious Research Center
  1985   Prayer in American Life. *Emerging Trends* 7:1–4.

17

Sacks, Howard L.
   1979   The Effect of Spiritual Exercises on the Integration of
          Self-System. *Journal for the Scientific Study of Religion*
          18:46–50.
Swatos, William H., Jr.
   1987   "The Power of Prayer: Observations and Possibilities."
          Pp. 103–14 in W.H. Swatos (ed). *Religious Sociology: Inter-*
          faces and Boundaries. New York: Greenwood Press.
Welford, A.T.
   1947   Is Religious Behavior Dependent upon Affect or Frustra-
          tion? *Journal of Abnormal and Social Psychology*
          42:310–19.

2

WHAT DO PEOPLE DO WHEN THEY PRAY?
Types of Prayer

> The immediate person thinks and imagines that when he prays, the important thing, the thing he must concentrate upon, is that *God should hear what he is praying for.* And yet in the true, eternal sense, it is just the reverse; the true relation in prayer is not when God hears what is prayed for, but when *the person praying continues to pray until he is* the one who hears, who hears what God wills. The immediate person, therefore, uses many words and, therefore, makes demands in his prayer; the true man of prayer only *attends.*
>
> — Søren Kierkegaard
> *Journal* (1846)

The English words "to pray" and "prayer" are derived from the Latin word *precare*, meaning "to ask for something" or "to beg." This origin explains the common understanding of the verb "to pray," which Webster's dictionary defines as "to make earnest petition." "To pray," however, has another given dictionary definition, namely, "to enter into spiritual communion with God."

Jean Daujat notes that these two distinct yet overlapping definitions may be explained by the fact that the Latin word *orare* is also translated as "to pray." *Orare* derives from *os*, the Latin word for mouth, and its primary meaning is not "to ask" but "to speak." Daujat (1964:8) continues:

> Thus, in its religious sense, prayer is an address directed to God or to a superior power in which we reveal our needs and implore that they be fulfilled. At the same time, the word takes on an added wealth of meaning: by prayer, in this religious sense, we mean not only the prayer of petition but any set of words addressed to some higher power, above all, to God, for example to thank him for benefits we have received and also to praise and admire him, to recognize him as Master and Lord of the universe. As soon as we grasp the true meaning of religion as an interior act of the soul, we realize that the value of prayer does not lie in the words themselves but in the interior attitude of soul which is expressed and revealed in words—an attitude of adoration, admiration, praise, recognition, love, confidence, hope, supplication.

The recognition that prayer involves diverse practices rather than a well-defined, monolithic ritual has been similarly noted by many other spiritual writers. Prayer is known to include adoration of God, thanksgiving for favors received, expressions of remorse for sin, or requests for material or spiritual favors. Taking different forms, prayer may be *rote*, involving recitation of prayer scripts; *conversational*, consisting of informally "talking to" God; or *affective*, a dialogue with God that is rooted in deeply felt convictions and goes beyond words. Prayer may be active, with the pray-er attempting to control the prayer dialogue; or it may be passive, with the pray-er patiently waiting for the action of God. As implied by the quotation by philosopher Søren Kierkegaard which was used to open this chapter, prayer involves a dialogue—not only speaking but also listening to God.

In constructing the questions used to measure prayer activities, we assumed diversity among pray-ers. We recognized that there were different forms of prayer activities and that some pray-ers used a wider range of practices than did others. To test our hypotheses, eleven questions were included in the Gallup survey to tap some of the assertions commonly made by spiritual writers on prayer. These prayer activities will be "typed" and then discussed briefly in light of the survey responses. Before taking a closer look at the types or forms of prayer which were derived from the survey responses, we will consider some of the demographic differences between the vast majority of those who claim to pray and those who never pray to God.

PRAYER IN SOCIAL CONTEXT

Consistent with Gallup findings for the past forty years, the results of the present survey indicate that nearly nine out of ten Americans pray to God. Eighty-eight percent of the 1988 respondents indicated that they, at least on occasion, did pray. Although differences among population groups are small, they are statistically significant. As may be seen in Table 1, men, those under twenty-five years of age, college graduates, whites, and those from the eastern section of the country are less likely to pray than women, those over sixty-five years of age, those with less than a high school degree, blacks, and those from the South. Eighty-five percent of the men but 91 percent of the women respondents claim to pray. Only 80 percent of those under under twenty-five but 91 percent of those over sixty-five claim to pray. Although 92 percent of Southerners say they pray to God, only 83 percent of Easterners similarly responded. A comparable pattern was found in an earlier Gallup survey which reported that while nationally 19 percent of Americans prayed three times a day or more, "the percentages for women, older persons, blacks, and Protestants are higher" (Gallup Report, 1987:42).

TABLE 1
Do You Ever Pray to God?

	Yes
Total (1,980 = weighted base)	88%
Sex	
Men (822)	85%
Women (916)	91%
Age	
18–24 (237)	80%
25–29 (223)	89%
30–49 (664)	88%
50–64 (296)	90%
65+ (306)	91%
Education	
Less than high school (388)	92%
High school graduate (537)	87%
Some college (452)	87%
College graduate (342)	85%
Race	
White (1,146)	87%
Non-white (252)	90%
Black (219)	94%
Hispanic (152)	84%
Region	
East (396)	83%
Midwest (419)	87%
South (567)	92%
West (356)	89%
Annual Income	
Under $15,000 (482)	87%
$15,000 to $25,000 (266)	82%
$25,000 to $40,000 (442)	88%
$40,000 and over (408)	92%

Additional questions may arise about what people do when then engage in behavior they call prayer. Some light may be shed on how people pray by considering some findings from the Akron Area Survey (AAS) not discussed in the last chapter. When pray-ers in the Akron sample were asked if they set aside a special time for prayer, only 43 percent responded affirmatively. The majority (57%) said they did not have a predesignated regular time for prayer.

The vast majority of the pray-ers (84%) at least on occasion coupled prayer with other daily activities. However, only a slight minority of the respondents (6%) limited their prayer to times in which they were engaged in activities such as working, driving, or exercising, with another 21 percent indicating that most of their prayer was combined with these exercises. A clear majority of the pray-ers (57%) described their combination of prayer with other activities as comprising only "some" of their praying.

Most personal prayer seems to be a solitary activity. Sixty-two percent of the pray-ers in AAS had never prayed informally with family members, church members, or friends; only 14 percent did so regularly. Of those who engaged in personal prayer with others (i.e., prayer outside of church activities and aside from prayers before meals), 52 percent prayed with their families, 61 percent with church members, and 48 percent with friends.

The social context of the modal private prayer appears to be an unscheduled time of solitude that is sometimes coupled with the performance of other activities. Relatively few persons, however, limit their prayer to formal set times. Even those who have scheduled a time for prayer are likely to supplement this prayer with less formal conversations with God. During the course of an interview,[1] a twenty-one-year old woman described her prayer style as follows:

1. Throughout this book quotations will be used at times to illustrate different facets of prayer. These quotations may come (as this one does) from interviews done

23

I always have a time of prayer (usually about ten or fifteen minutes just before I go to sleep at night) during which I pray on my knees. But really I try to pray all during the day. I call these my "popcorn prayers"—I pray whatever pops into my head. And all kinds of things pop into my head. Sometimes I see a beautiful sunset and just need to praise God. Or I've just missed getting hit by another car changing lanes on the expressway and I need to thank him. Or maybe I just need to tell God that I love him. I don't have to be in some quiet and secluded place on my knees to make contact with God. Prayer can occur anywhere because God is always with me.

As this quotation indicates, what we call prayer entails a variety of activities—activities that were represented by eleven questions on our survey. The findings that follow on the types or forms of prayer are based on the responses of the 88 percent of the sample who acknowledged that prayer was a part of their lives.

TYPING PRAYER ACTIVITIES

Given what devotional writers have indicated about prayer, we had reason to assume our eleven questions about prayer activities could be reduced to a few common denominators. To verify this assumption empirically, the questions were submitted to a statistical procedure known as "factor analysis," which seeks to determine whether some questions share a common, underlying meaning, or "load" on a single factor. Our questions "loaded" on four factors—what we have called *ritual prayer, conversational prayer, petitionary prayer*, and *medita-*

---

with a non-random sample of people about their prayer lives, from research projects done by Margaret Poloma (1989) (primarily on members of the Assemblies of God and while doing field research on the rural poor in Kentucky), or from autobiographical published accounts. Although one cannot generalize from such a nonsystematic sample, the quotations are used to enhance the reader's understanding of the kinds of attitudes and behavior represented by our survey questions.

tive prayer. Table 2 provides the breakdown for the questions and the percent of respondents responding positively to each question.

Ritual Prayer

Ritual prayer activities are one type of verbal prayer which may be likened to reading or reciting a prepared script. They include the Catholic practice of saying the rosary, reading prayers that appear in daily devotionals, and reciting prayers that have been committed to memory. Two questions were used to tap this form of prayer: Do you read from a book of prayers? and Do you recite memorized prayers?

Of the 911 or 88 percent of the persons who responded affirmatively to the question "Do you ever pray to God?" 22 percent at least on occasion used a prayer book for prayer. The vast majority (78%) did not. Half of those who prayed (50%) at least occasionally recited memorized prayers. Nineteen percent of those who prayed used *both* memorized prayers and a prayer book as a means of communicating with God.

Perhaps not surprising is the finding that older persons were significantly more likely to employ ritual prayers than were younger persons. Twenty-seven percent of those over sixty-five years of age but only 16 percent of those under age twenty-five scored high on ritual prayer, indicating that they both recited memorized prayers and used a prayer book. Other demographic factors, including income, education, sex, and marital status, were not statistically related to ritual prayer.

Another significant difference that may be found in Table 3 between those who used ritual prayer and those who did not is denominational affiliation. Protestants were less likely than Catholics both to read from a book of prayers and to recite memorized prayers. Twenty-nine percent of the Catholic respondents but only 16 percent of the total Protestant sample ever used a prayer book. The difference is also pronounced

TABLE 2
Forms of Prayer

	Yes
Total respondents = 1,030; weighted base = 1,980	
1. Do you ever pray to God?	88%
To those who respond yes to question 1:	
2. When you pray, are you likely to	
Ritual Prayer (% answering "yes" on both items)	19%
Read from a book of prayers	21%
Recite prayers you have memorized	50%
Petitionary Prayer (% answering "yes" on single item)	42%
Ask God for material things you may need	42%
Conversational Prayer (% answering "yes" on four items)	84%
Talk with God in your own words	95%
Ask God to forgive your sins	91%
Ask God to provide guidance in making decisions	90%
Thank God for his blessings	96%
Meditative Prayer (% answering "yes" on four items)	52%
Spend time quietly thinking about God	75%
Spend time just "feeling" the presence of God	65%
Spend time worshiping and adoring God	68%
Try to listen to God speak to you	70%

TABLE 3
Ritual Prayer

When you pray, are you likely to

Read from a book of prayers (22% = yes)

Age	Yes
18–24	18%
25–29	16%
30–49	20%
50–64	23%
65+	29%

Denomination	Yes	Race	Yes
Catholic	29%	White	20%
Total Protestant	16%	Non-white	27%
Evangelical	14%	Black	25%
Non-evangelical	25%	Hispanic	38%

Recite prayers you have memorized (50% = yes)

Age	Yes
18–24	51%
25–29	40%
30–49	49%
50–64	53%
65 +	56%

Denomination	Yes	Race	Yes
Catholic	72%	White	49%
Total Protestant	40%	Non-white	55%
Evangelical	38%	Black	53%
Non-evangelical	55%	Hispanic	59%

NOTE: Income, education, and sex do not show a statistically significant, relationship with ritual prayer items.

when comparing figures within Protestantism: only 14 percent of the evangelicals read from a book of prayers while 25 percent of non-evangelical Christians reported doing so.

The persons most likely to rely on ritual prayer are older Catholics. Traditionally Catholics have been encouraged to use prayer books and to memorize prayers ranging from the Morning Offering (offering one's day to God), the Angelus (a prayer commemorating the annunciation that is said three times a day), to a formalized act of contrition (recited by the penitent during confession). Although private ritual prayer is less emphasized in the post–Vatican II Catholic church, certain devotionals are still very common. A particularly popular Catholic devotion which dates back to the Middle Ages is the recitation of the rosary.[2] Interviews with Catholics who recite the rosary suggest that it may be a rote ritual at times, but often it sets the stage for other prayer forms. In the words of one fifty-six-year-old respondent:

> There are times I need to make contact with God, but he seems very far away. During those times I'll force myself to recite the rosary—and somehow he'll just become present. After I finish the decades I can go on to talk with him in my own words. I don't understand how it works, I just know that it does.

Whether ritual prayer involves saying the rosary, reciting prayers written by others, or reading from the book of Psalms, it most frequently is practiced as only one form of prayer. For some it may be described more as a ritual practice than a com-

---

2. The rosary is a practice that involves prayer repetitions while thinking about assigned "mysteries" or events connected with the lives of Jesus or Mary. The complete rosary involves the recitation of 150 Hail Marys (a prayer to Mary that begins with the Angel Gabriel's greeting found in Luke 1:28-32). The Hail Marys are grouped into decades with an Our Father (the Lord's Prayer) recited before each group of ten Hail Marys. Each decade in turn represents a "mystery" or one of fifteen commemorative events such as Gabriel's apparition to Mary to announce Jesus' birth, Jesus' crucifixion, or Jesus' bodily ascension into heaven.

munion with God; for most it is coupled with or actually facilitates (as the previous quotation suggests) other types of prayer activities.

Ritual prayer is the least popular of the prayer types, particularly for evangelical Protestant pray-ers. When Protestants do acknowledge the use of memorized prayers, most often they refer to a recitation of the psalms or some other biblical passage. Catholics, on the other hand, draw from a host of memorized prayers, including the Act of Contrition, the Angelus, the Hail Mary, the Morning Offering, and the rosary. Despite such differences in content, the ritual prayer form is employed by a significant group of pray-ers, especially Catholics and older persons, often as a prelude to other forms of prayer.

Conversational Prayer

Apparently most people who pray do not use or do not limit themselves to reading from prayer books or reciting memorized texts. Most couple it with the most popular of the prayer types, what we have called "colloquial," or "conversational," prayer which incorporates four activities. Ninety-five percent of those who pray say that they do talk to God in their own words. These informal conversations may revolve around different themes. Loading on the same factor with the question about "talking to God" were three other questions identifying some of these themes: "Do you ask God to forgive your sins?" "Do you thank God for his blessings?" and "Do you ask God to provide guidance in making decisions?" Ninety-two percent of those who prayed asked God to forgive their sins, 91 percent asked God for guidance in making decisions, and 78 percent prayed prayers of thanksgiving.

A twenty-five-year-old male college student made the following comment about his prayer life during an interview. It illustrates well the interface among the specific activities we have called conversational prayer:

I pray when I get up in the morning and just before I go to bed. But I don't limit myself to these two five to twenty minute prayer times. I talk to God all through the day. I pray frequently during the day, often to thank him for his blessings. When I am happy, I thank God for life and whatever it is that is making me happy. I really feel compelled to pray when times are tough. I believe it's through these tough times that a person is drawn closer to God. When I feel boxed in and need direction, I ask God for his guidance. When I feel I've said something or done something I should not have, I tell God I am sorry. Most of these prayers are silent—done in conversational style in my heart.

Eighty-four percent of the survey respondents who prayed engaged in all four of the conversational prayer activities, with another 11 percent responding affirmatively to three of the four questions. Like the young man whose quotation we have just read, most respondents moved easily from talking generally with God, to seeking guidance or forgiveness, to praying in thanksgiving. Only 5 percent of the pray-ers employed only two or one of the practices. Conversational prayer may be regarded as a kind of generic prayer form with virtually no socio-demographic differences; almost everyone who claims to pray engages in it.

Although it involves a less formal method than ritual prayer, there is some indication that conversational prayer may share a quality of more formal ritualistic prayer activities. Like ritual prayer, conversational prayer may be a monologue rather than a dialogue. It may involve perceived dialogue with God *or* it may be set and routine. For example, although 91 percent of the respondents requested divine guidance for decision making, nearly half (43%) had never experienced God's leading them to perform a specific action, and a little over a quarter (28%) reported they had never received an answer from God to a specific prayer request. Apparently, for some respondents conversational prayer may involve a dialogue with God; for others, it may be a one-way monologue with a God who seemingly does not respond.

Jean-Claude Sagne (1972:19) has described "the practice of prayer as talking to God" paradoxically as a possible "obstacle to meeting with the living and true God and the hearing of his word of power." Sagne elaborates:

> Unknown to himself, the worshipper may construct a sort of spiritual atheism in which representations of God and types of prayer become too infiltrated by the imagination and become defenses against the presence of God and obstacles to his free intervention. Even the language of prayer may deteriorate into noise and blur the word of God, which can only be heard in silence.

Conversational pray-ers may have moved to a less formal type of prayer, but they have not necessarily learned the art of listening to God in silent waiting.

Petitionary Prayer

Petitionary prayer may be one of the most difficult prayer forms for modern men and women. Christian Duquoc and Claude Geffré (1972:8) describe prayers of petition to be in a state of crisis "brought about by scientific and technical power over nature." Science and technology stimulate a different understanding of prayer for many people that does not include asking for material things. Josef Brommer (1972:73) describes some of the criticisms leveled against petitionary prayer as follows:

> The prayer of petition is criticized by scientists, who regard it as a purely illusory faith in God's providence which contradicts the laws of natural science. The psychological objection is that prayer is based on an egocentric assumption that God's control of the world is dependent on the desires of the person praying, who can in this way, gain power over God. Prayer originally meant "exercising

power", was closely related to the practice of magic and laid claims to God himself.

Comments volunteered by some who were interviewed during the time we were analyzing the survey data similarly reflected a negative attitude toward petitionary prayer. Respondents often said they would ask God only to help them *to do* the things they needed to do in order to secure what they wanted. Some were quick to quote the familiar American adage, "God helps those who help themselves." Others insisted that praying for material needs was selfish and childish. A twenty-four-year-old female student commented:

> I think praying for material things is usually selfish. I try not to ask for new clothes, cars or things like that. I have on occasion asked God to guide me so I might earn the money for things that are necessary to survive. I used to pray for specific things when I was little, but as I got older I felt such prayers were childish and selfish.

Despite such criticisms, Jesus himself taught his followers to ask for what they needed, as represented by the "give us this day, our daily bread" petition of the Lord's Prayer. Interviewees who objected to the use of petitionary prayer seemed to do so for two primary reasons: (1) such prayer tends to be self-centered and immature, and (2) petitionary prayer requires an image of a God who is willing and able to intervene in the daily affairs of humans. Other respondents who believed in the power of petitionary prayer were able to provide testimonies of tangible blessings they believed were the result of prayerful intercession. As we shall demonstrate through our survey results, those who employ petitionary prayer tend to score higher on other forms of prayer and general religiosity measures than those who do not.

The question that was used to represent petitionary prayer asked about praying for material things that the respondent may need.[3] Apparently not all requests to God are the same. Earlier research (Poloma and Pendleton, 1989, 1991) based on the Akron Area Survey demonstrates that praying for material things appears to be a distinct form of petitioning, while praying for nonmaterial needs appears to be a facet of general conversational prayer.

Only 42 percent of the respondents acknowledged that they ever prayed for material things. As may be seen from the results presented in Table 4, black respondents were nearly twice as likely to engage in this form of petitionary prayer than were whites (66% versus 38%). In general it appears that those who are most likely to have material needs, those with less than a high school education, and those with an income under $15,000 a year are more likely than college graduates and those with greater incomes to ask God for material things.

There is some indication, however, that material deprivation is not the only catalyst for such prayer. Although petitionary prayer is sometimes deprecated, it takes a great deal of faith to make requests for tangible objects. A person can never be certain that his or her sins are forgiven or that God has heard a prayer of thanksgiving, but a concrete prayer for a better job or money to pay a bill can be verified. Persons who pray for material things they may need are likely to score higher on other religiosity measures. For example, they are more likely to report that religion is very important to them, that they are members of a church, and that they are "born-again." Evangelicals, a group of Christians who consistently score higher on religiosity measures, are significantly more likely to engage in

3. Although three of the "prayer-activities" questions asked in the survey may be considered petitionary items, statistical analysis failed to place these three items in the same category. Those petitions which were less tangible, namely, praying for divine guidance and asking for the forgiveness of sins, failed to cluster with the question, "Do you ask God for material things you may need?" This same pattern was found in the Akron Area Survey, with one other item that was not included in the present survey (praying for material things which friends or relatives may need).

TABLE 4
Petitionary Prayer

When you pray, are you likely to

Ask God for material things you may need? (42% = yes)

Age	Yes
18–24	40%
25–29	36%
30–49	39%
50–64	46%
65+	50%

Denomination	Yes	Race	Yes
Catholic	37%	White	38%
Total Protestant	48%	Non-white	65%
Evangelical	59%	Black	66%
Non-evangelical	31%	Hispanic	44%

Income	Yes	Education	Yes
Under $15,000	53%	Less than high school	50%
$15,000–$25,000	45%	High school graduate	43%
$25,000–$40,000	39%	Some college	40%
Over $40,000	31%	College graduate	35%

NOTE: Sex is not a significantly related category to petitionary prayer.

---

petitionary prayer than other Protestants (59% as compared with 31%). Need coupled with a viable faith seem to be strongly correlated with this prayer form.

A young mother of three living in rural Kentucky came to mind while writing this section. Emma Lou, a young woman in her early thirties, lived in a remote rural area in an old trailer house without running water. She was unemployed, her husband was in prison, and she was forced to rely on neighbors for transportation to town. Yet Emma Lou seemed to have a serenity about her as she tried to manage food and fuel bills for herself and her children. She commented:

> I have to depend on God. There ain't nobody else to turn to. When we have no money for food, I ask Him to provide for me. He always does. Just one day last month I had no money and no food. A man in a pick-up truck pulled up to the trailer and unloaded six boxes of groceries. I didn't know who he was—still don't. I believe it was God that sent him.

Emma Lou shared other incidents—incidents that she believed were more than "coincidences," that were, rather, God's intervention in her life as a result of petitionary prayer. Others may focus on naturalistic explanations, but for Emma Lou and countless others God is the one who sends the bearer of the gifts. For many believers in petitionary prayer, God indeed does hear their cries for help and provides them with concrete answers.

Meditative Prayer

The types of prayer discussed above have differing characteristics and vary in the degree to which they are practiced by American pray-ers, yet they appear to have a common characteristic. All are active forms of prayer, ranging from using prayer formulae to informal prayer oriented toward petitioning some material or spiritual blessing. The four items that factored together for what we are calling *meditative prayer* appear to require less activity and more passivity on the part of the pray-er. These are (1) spending time quietly thinking about God, (2) "feeling" the presence of God, (3) worshiping and adoring God, and (4) trying to listen to God speaking.

All four items included in the meditative prayer scale were practiced by 52 percent of American pray-ers—a lower percentage than those involved in conversational prayer but a higher percent than indicated by ritual and petitional prayer scores. Sixty-eight percent of those who prayed spent time worshiping and adoring God; 70 percent tried to listen for God's voice; 66 percent spent time just feeling the presence of God; and 75 percent included times of quietly thinking about God in their prayer lives. Only 8 percent of pray-ers did not engage in any meditative prayer activities. Interviews seem to indicate that this more passive form of prayer is often preceded by ritual, conversational, or petitionary prayer. Meditative prayer seems to represent a more advanced form of praying which is a regular practice only after other forms of prayer. A middle-aged woman whom we will call Jean has been praying for at least one and a half hours a day for the last twenty years. She described her prayer journey as follows:

> I learned to pray from my mother. At first most of my prayers were needs-based—not just for material things but for help in dealing with people and problems. Most of my prayer time now is spent praising and worshiping God. He is so very present when I praise Him! I may begin by reciting some passages, especially the Psalms. Other times I may just sit and think about God. He comes and is present to me. But my experience of God is not limited to the time I set aside for prayer. The Holy Spirit leads me throughout the day. Prayer is a part of me—perhaps the most important part.

Talking further with Jean about her prayer life made it clear that meditative pray-ers also employ other forms of prayer. Reading the psalms may be classified as ritual prayer, but it is not mechanistic for Jean. Jean still asks for "my daily bread," but petitionary prayer is not as central to her prayer life as it once was. Jean often talks to God in her own words, but she has learned to listen to God as well as to just be still and know that he is God.

There are important demographic differences between those who have moved beyond vocal active prayer to a more silent, passive type. As reported in Table 5, there appear to be a number of demographic differences between high and low scorers on meditative prayer. Statistically significant and linear relationships exist between meditative prayer and age, income, and education. As people age, they appear more likely to be involved in meditative prayer. Those with lower income and less education are also more likely to engage in passive forms of prayer. Women are significantly more likely to be meditative pray-ers than are men.

It appears that those who may be less in control of their personal lives—the elderly, those with less education, women, and those with less income—are more likely to be able to take the quiet and passive stance demanded by meditative prayer. Interestingly, this form of prayer, unlike ritual prayer and petitionary prayer, does not seem to be affected by denominational affiliation or by race.

Thomas Merton, the late Trappist monk whose works are known by many both inside and outside the Catholic community, claimed that meditative prayer may be termed "prayer of the heart"—"at least in the sense of prayer that seeks its roots in the very ground of our being, not merely in our mind or our affections" (Merton, 1969:34). He goes on to note:

> In the "prayer of the heart" we seek first of all the deepest ground of our identity in God. We do not reason about dogmas or faith, or "the mysteries." We seek rather to gain a direct existential grasp, a personal experience of the deepest truths of life and faith, *finding ourselves in God's truth*. . . . *Prayer* then means yearning for the simple presence of God, for a personal understanding of his word, for knowledge of his will and for capacity to hear and obey him. It is thus something much more than uttering petitions for good things external to our own deepest concerns. (Merton, 1969:82–83)

TABLE 5
Meditative Prayer°

When you pray are you likely to

Spend time quietly thinking about God?
Spend time just "feeling" the presence of God?
Spend time worshiping and adoring God?
Try to listen to God speak to you?

Sex	High	Age	High
Men	48%	18–24	45%
Women	59%	25–29	47%
		30–49	45%
		50–64	52%
		65+	70%

Annual Income	High	Education	High
Less than $15,000	61%	Less than high school	66%
$15,000–$25,000	62%	High school graduate	53%
$25,000–$40,000	50%	Some college	50%
Over $40,000	41%	College graduate	44%

NOTE: Race and denomination were not statistically significant to meditative prayer.

°Meditative prayer includes the four prayer activity items listed above. Fifty-two percent of those who prayed engaged in all four activities. Data reported in Table 5 represent the descriptive statistics for those who scored "high" in meditative prayer. The "low" scorers were the 16 percent who said "yes" to three out of four of the items; 14 percent, two out of four; 11 percent, one out of four; and 8 percent who did not engage in any of the meditative prayer activities.

It would appear that meditative prayer has the most potential for a dialogue with God. Although meditative pray-ers inevitably use other prayer forms, especially conversational but quite possibly petitionary and ritual prayer techniques as well, they supplement these more active forms of prayer with a more passive stance. They have, in varying degrees, learned to move beyond the chatter of more active forms of prayer toward a paradoxically silent and passive dialogue.

PRAYER AND RELATIONSHIP
WITH GOD

Before closing this chapter, we would like to test the hypothesis that meditative prayer does allow for more perceived dialogue with God than do the more active prayer forms. To do this, we will briefly consider the relationship between the four types of prayer and a perceived closeness to God.

In order to tap respondents' perceptions of their relationship with God, the following question was included in the Gallup survey: "Where on this scale of 1 to 7, with 1 being very distant and 7 being very close, would you describe your relationship with God?" Nineteen percent of the respondents indicated a distant relationship, choosing numbers 1, 2, or 3. Seventeen percent selected the median number. The majority, 60 percent, chose 5, 6, or 7, indicating a close relationship. Some 20 percent of the respondents selected 7, describing a very close relationship; 4 percent responded with "don't know."

All four of the types of prayer were positively related to feeling close to God, but there were differences in the strength of that relationship. Bivariate correlations indicate that the meditative prayer scale shows the strongest relationship with a felt closeness to God, while conversational prayer, petitionary prayer, and ritual prayer show much weaker relationships.[4] Put another way, the quiet and passive practice of meditative prayer is very likely to be the prayer form of those who report feeling closest to God—more likely than the more verbal and active colloquial, ritual, or petitionary modes of praying. Yet bivariate relationships tell only part of the story.

Most people engage in more than one form of prayer, and such bivariate analysis does not permit us to control for actual differences related to the respective prayer forms. Using a procedure known as "multiple regression" allows us to sort out the differences which may be attributed to each type of prayer activity. When all four prayer types are entered into a single multiple regression equation, only meditative prayer still demonstrates a positive relationship with feeling close to God. When the demographics of race, income, education, age, and denomination are added to this same equation, meditative prayer retains its position as the best predictor of such closeness.

Put into descriptive terms, this multiple regression equation says that those who engage in ritual, petitionary, and/or conversational prayer *but who do not also use a meditative prayer form* are less likely to feel very close to God. Conversational, ritual, or petitionary pray-ers who are not involved in meditative prayer do not report feeling the deeper union with God enjoyed by the more passive pray-ers. In the words of Jesuit spiritual writer George Maloney (1983:13), meditative prayer moves the pray-er "away from this or that act that you are in charge of to enter into a more total experience of oneness with God." According to Maloney and other spiritual writers,

4. The Pearsonian correlation for meditative prayer and having a close relationship with God is .43. The other zero-order correlations are as follows: conversational prayer, $r = .25$; ritual prayer, $r = .15$; and petitionary prayer, $r = .14$. The results of multivariate analysis indicate that meditative prayer is in fact the prayer form that contributes to accounting for a closer relationship with God. When all four types of prayer are entered into a single multiple regression equation, only meditative prayer (beta = .39) shows a statistically significant relationship with perceived closeness to God.

God is then able to break through and persons come to experience God dwelling within them.

Chapter 3 will continue to explore the four types of prayer, but this time with the focus on prayer experiences. Do pray-ers actually experience the God to whom they pray? Are the prayer types described in this chapter related to the believer's experiences of God? The relationship between religious experiences during private prayer and the types of prayer will be further explored in the following chapter.

WORKS CITED

Brommer, Josef
    1972   Is the Prayer of Petition and Intercession Still Meaningful?
            In *The Prayer Life*, edited by Christian Duquoc and Claude
            Geffré, pp. 73–82. New York: Herder and Herder.
Daujat, Jean
    1964   *Prayer*. Translated by Martin Murphy. New York: Hawthorn Books.
Duquoc, Christian, and Claude Geffré, eds.
    1972   *The Prayer Life*. New York: Herder and Herder.
Gallup Report
    1987   *Religion in America*. Princeton, N.J.: The Gallup Organization.
Maloney, George A.
    1983   *Journey into Contemplation*. Locust Valley, N.Y.: Living
            Flame Press.
Merton, Thomas
    1969   *Contemplative Prayer*. New York: Herder and Herder.
Poloma, Margaret
    1989   *The Assemblies of God at the Crossroads: Charisma and
            Institutional Dilemmas*. Knoxville: University of Tennessee
            Press.
Poloma, Margaret M., and Brian F. Pendleton
    1989   Exploring Types of Prayer and the Quality of Life. *Review
            of Religious Research* 31 (September):46–53

1991   The Effects of Prayer and Prayer Experiences on Measures of General Well-Being. *Journal of Psychology and Theology* 19(1):71–83.

Sagne, Jean-Claude
1972   Coming to Terms with the Father: Prayer and Psychoanalysis. In *The Prayer Life*, edited by Christian Duquoc and Claude Geffré, pp. 15–25. New York: Herder and Herder.

3

DOES GOD REALLY SPEAK?
Religious Experiences during Prayer

[I]n effect what I have been saying is that the evidence from the peak-experiences permits us to talk about the essential, the intrinsic, the basic, the most fundamental religious or transcendent experience as a totally private and personal one which can hardly be shared (except with other "peakers"). As a consequence, all the paraphernalia of organized religion— buildings and specialized personnel, rituals, dogmas, ceremonials, and the like—are to the "peaker" secondary, peripheral, and of doubtful value in relation to the intrinsic and essential religious or transcendent experience.

— Abraham H. Maslow (1964:28)

Abraham Maslow, the late humanistic psychologist, well known for his theory of the "hierarchy of needs," challenged social scientists to study religious experiences in his lesser known work on religions and peak experiences. His basic thesis was that while all great religions were the product of prophets and seers who had intense peak experiences, the institutions that developed around them and their teachings were inimical to the very experiences that birthed those institutions. Maslow asserts that this is due to a "form of idolatry" which concretizes the statues, ceremonies, and symbols rather than the original revelation. As he states:

> In idolatry the essential original meaning gets so lost in concretizations that these finally become hostile to the original mystical experiences, to mystics, and to prophets in general, that is, to the very people that we might call from our present point of view the truly religious people. Most religions have wound up denying and being antagonistic to the very ground upon which they were originally based. (Maslow, 1964:24)

While Maslow has written an intriguing and thought provoking book, few have picked up on his challenge of studying religious experiences—particularly those of a more garden variety. Studies have been done on drug-induced mysticism and other esoteric topics, but not on religious counterparts of Maslow's peak experiences.[1] Maslow found peak experiences to be commonplace and implied that religious experiences are not limited to the celebrated mystics who reportedly see visions and hear voices. By including questions reflecting what may be regarded as common mysticism, the Gallup data provides an opportunity to explore Maslow's thesis.

A TAXONOMY OF
RELIGIOUS EXPERIENCE

Religious experiences may be defined as perceived encounters between the pray-er and God. In other words, they may be regarded as interpersonal encounters that involve a sense of intimacy. Rodney Stark (1965:99) suggests that religious experience may be conceived of as a dyadic form of interaction—"the divinity and the individual as a pair of actors involved in a social encounter." When viewed in this way, some

---

1. For an excellent review of psychological research on religious experiences, see Chapter 7 in Spilka, Hood, and Gorsuch (1985).

general configurations of relations between God and the person at prayer can be ordered in terms of social distance. Stark identifies four such possible configurations:

1. The human actor simply notes (feels, senses, etc.) the existence or presence of the divine actor.
2. Mutual presence is acknowledged; the divine actor is perceived as noting the presence of the human actor.
3. The awareness of mutual presence is replaced by an affective relationship akin to love or friendship.
4. The human actor perceives himself as a confidant of and/or a fellow participant in action with the divine actor.

Stark notes that in normal human affairs one has more acquaintances than friends, and even fewer intimate relations. He convincingly demonstrates that a similar pattern holds in religious encounters. The more intimate relationship of the fourth configuration requires passing through the less intimate previous states. Correspondingly, the earlier states are more widespread in the population than are the later states.

The five questions used to measure religious experiences correspond to the taxonomy developed by Rodney Stark. The vast majority of the pray-ers (89%) reported they had experienced a deep sense of peace and well-being during prayer. A somewhat fewer number (79%) "felt the strong presence of God" during personal prayer. An even smaller percentage of respondents perceived not only that they were aware of God but that God acknowledges them. Seventy-two percent reported receiving at least once what they regarded as a definite answer to a specific prayer request. A somewhat deeper awareness of this mutual presence may be reflected in the question which asks about receiving insights into spiritual truths during prayer. Only 61 percent of the pray-ers claimed to have ever had that experience. The least reported of the prayer experiences was the item tapping the pray-er's perception of being a fellow participant in action with God. Only 57 percent claimed to have ever had the experience of feeling "divinely inspired or 'led by God' to perform some specific action as a result of prayer." Each of these prayer experiences will be considered further as illuminated by the survey data.

Sensing the Divine Actor through a Feeling of Peace

> Peace I leave with you; my peace I give you. I do not give to you as the world gives. Do not let your hearts be troubled and do not be afraid. (John 14:27)

Wishing the peace of God upon another is a frequent biblical salutation. It apparently is something that those who pray experience with some relative frequency. In an earlier Gallup survey that sought to learn the effects of prayer, respondents were asked how prayer affects their thoughts or actions (*Emerging Trends*, 1985). The most likely responses were, "It makes me feel good" and "It gives me peace of mind." The present survey reflects the same finding, namely, that a sense of peace and well-being is the most common reward of prayer. As may be seen in Table 1, 32 percent of all pray-ers claim regularly to have a sense of peace and well-being during prayer. Twelve percent are classified as never having had such an experience, 9 percent reporting a negative response and another 3 percent being "uncertain" (which probably implies they have not had or felt such peace).

Sensing the existence of God through a feeling of deep peace seems to be the near-universal prayer experience. Yet there were some socio-demographic differences, the summary results of which may be seen in the correlations shown in Table 2. The profile of the person most likely to experience a sense of

TABLE 1
Prayer Experiences°

The next questions are about some experiences that you might have had during prayer. How often have you experienced the following?

	Never[+]	Once or twice	Occasionally	Regularly
Experienced a deep sense of peace and well-being	12%	19%	38%	32%
Felt the strong presence of God	21%	20%	33%	26%
Received what you regarded as a definite answer to a specific prayer request	27%	25%	32%	15%
Received what you believed to be a deeper insight into a spiritual or biblical truth	39%	21%	28%	12%
Felt divinely inspired or "led by God" to perform some specific action	43%	22%	26%	9%

°Percentages may add up to more than 100% due to rounding. Based on those 911 respondents who ever pray to God: weighted base = 1,738.

[+] "Never" includes those who "did not know" or "were not certain," as well as those who gave a negative response to the questions.

peace during prayer is that of an older female who defines herself as a born-again Christian. Although men and women prayers are equally likely to report having experienced a deep sense of peace during prayer, women are more likely to report *regular* experiences (38% versus 25%). Respondents between the ages of twenty-two and forty-two (the "baby boomers") were less likely to experience peace during prayer than those over age sixty-five (12% of the first category but only 6% of the second group *never* experience such peace). Although 48 percent of evangelical pray-ers have regular experiences of a deep sense of peace, only 24 percent of the non-evangelical respondents made such a claim. These differences should not eclipse the fact that sensing the peace of God seems to be a basic religious experience with which nearly every person who prays can identify.

TABLE 2
Bivariate Correlations for
Experiences of God during Private Prayer
with Select Variables

	Age	Education	Income	Evangelical[+]	Sex	Race
Sense of Peace	.11	.06°	ns	-.28	.11	ns
Presence of God	.13	ns	ns	-.35	.13	ns
Answered Prayer	.16	ns	ns	-.35	.17	ns
Deeper Spiritual Truth	ns	ns	ns	-.34	.07°	ns
Divine Leading	.17	-.05°	ns	-.31	.07°	.09°
PRAYER EXPERIENCE SCALE	.15	ns	ns	-.37	.13	ns

°Correlations are significant between .01 and .05; all other reported correlations are significant at the .001 level.

[+]Evangelicals were coded as born-again = 1; not born-again = 2.
Sex was coded as men = 1; women = 2.
Race was coded as white = 1; black = 2.
ns = not significant

Sensing the Presence of God

Blessed are those who have learned to acclaim you, who walk in the light of your presence, O Lord. They rejoice in your name all day long; they exult in your righteousness. (Ps. 89:15–16)

Sensing God's presence does not take a single form, as may be seen from accounts of intensely mystical, Judeo-Christian experiences reported in the Bible. So intense was Isaiah's experience (Isa. 6:5) that he cried out that he was "ruined" after encountering the Almighty God. In contrast, Elijah's experience of God was as a "gentle whisper" (1 Kings 19:11). Moses' encounter of God in the burning bush was coupled with the instructions to take off his sandals "for the place where you are standing is holy ground" (Exod. 3:5). Jacob's encounter with God is described as a wrestling match with a stranger (Gen. 32:30). The descriptions of such experiences of God's presence are as diverse as the prophets and seers who reported them.

The present survey made no attempt to use such rich and descriptive biblical imagery but rather simply asked respondents if they had ever had a strong sense of the presence of God during prayer. Twenty-six percent of those who prayed said that the experience of a strong sense of the presence of God was a regular occurrence (Table 1). Another 33 percent reported having this experience occasionally, with an additional 20 percent having had it only "once or twice." As may be seen from the figures reported in Table 1, there is a drop in both the number of respondents reporting the experience of the presence of God and the number who regularly have this experience.

If one judges from comments made by our non-random sample of interviewees, sensing the presence of God may take different forms. Most frequently its occurrences were more representative of Elijah's "gentle whisper" than the accounts of

Isaiah, Moses, or Jacob. One thirty-five-year-old woman described one of her experiences as feeling "all warm—like God had wrapped me up in a blanket and was holding me close to him." Feelings of warmth were often noted, as was a tingling sensation which ran through the body as a gentle current. Such feelings may be accompanied by a loss of the sense of physical and spatial boundaries. One middle-aged businessman commented:

> I try to settle my spirit when I first come to prayer by sitting quietly with my eyes closed and letting go of my thoughts one by one as they arise. Usually—sooner or later—I feel empty and full at the same time. Empty of the business that usually fills my life, but full of a tranquil presence I can't really describe. Once this happens I am oblivious to my surroundings, indifferent to time and place. I seem to be filled with a transparent light that leaves me as content as a baby who has just been fed.

Our survey data suggests that not all groups of pray-ers are equally likely to sense the divine presence during prayer. As may be seen from the Pearsonian correlations provided in Table 2, differences may be found based on age, sex, and evangelical orientation.

These correlations may be illustrated through percentages *not* provided in Table 2. Twenty-one percent of those between the ages of twenty-two and forty-two had never felt the strong presence of God during prayer, but only 14 percent of those over sixty-five years of age fell into this category. Women were significantly more likely to report a regular sensing of God's presence in prayer than were men (32% as compared with 18%). Evangelicals were considerably more likely to report a regular experience of God's presence than were non-evangelicals (43% as compared with 17%). Catholics, who were less likely to report a "born-again experience" (and thus be labeled "evangelical"), were also more likely than Protestants *never* to have felt the strong presence of God in prayer (21% versus 13%). Not surprisingly, church attenders were nearly twice as likely to report regular experiences of God's presence than were nonattenders (35% versus 18%). No other sociodemographic variables were found to be related to this prayer experience. Education, race and income were not statistically related to this measure of religious experience.

Divine-Human Interaction through Answered Prayer

> And I tell you, Ask, and it will be given you; seek, and you will find; knock and it will be opened to you. For every one who asks receives, and he who seeks finds; and to him who knocks it will be opened. (Luke 11:9–10)

Although a sense of the Divine Other may be experienced through peace or through sensing God's presence, interaction may or may not be present. One may be in a room with another person, know the person is present, but not engage in any form of interaction. Similarly, the pray er may be talking with God and may sense a divine presence, but the intimacy of interaction may be lacking. The next question, *asking* and *knowing one has received* an answer to a prayer request (Table 1), implies more of an interactive process. The pray-er has addressed the Divine and feels he or she has heard from God in the form of answered prayer.

Answered prayer covers a wide range of petitions that may be subdivided into praying for material needs and nonmaterial concerns. Whereas petitioning for nonmaterial concerns, including forgiveness of sin and divine guidance, is a practice of nearly all pray-ers in the sample, less than half acknowledged praying for personal material needs.[2] Our interviews suggest

2. Ninety-one percent of the respondents who prayed did so to petition God for forgiveness of sin, and 89 percent prayed for divine guidance in decision making. Only 44 percent ever prayed for material things that they needed.

that these material needs include petitions ranging from parking places to a job; from finding lost objects to requests for physical healing. The infrequency with which people allegedly petition for concrete needs lends support to an assertion made by Metropolitan Anthony Bloom in *Living Prayer*: "On our level of half-belief it is easier to sing hymns of praise or to thank God than to trust God enough to ask something with faith." To that we would add, that it is easier to ask God to help with non-material concerns than to provide for concrete material needs. Although most people have at some time experienced answered prayer, such answers are reported to be "regular" by only 15 percent of the respondents.

A significant number of respondents who prayed never received an answer to a specific request, whether in the form of concrete material needs or answers to spiritual concerns. Twenty-two percent of those who pray have never experienced receiving an answer to a specific prayer request, with an additional 5 percent being uncertain. Another 25 percent have had this experience only on one or two occasions. Only 15 percent of the pray-ers claimed regularly to experience receiving answers to specific prayer requests.

There were some significant group differences between those who received answers to prayer and those who did not. Men were more likely to report *never* having had this experience than were women (32% versus 23%), and women were more likely to be *regular* recipients of answered prayer than were men (20% as compared with 10%). Although the overall correlations for education and race are not statistically significant, our analysis shows that those making more than $40,000 a year are more likely to never have had a specific prayer request answered than were those making less than $15,000 (17% versus 29%), and white pray-ers were somewhat less likely regularly to have this experience than were blacks (15% as compared with 21%). Only 13 percent of those over age sixty-five had never had a specific prayer answered while

30 percent of the "baby boom" contingent between the ages of twenty-two and forty-two reported never having experienced answered prayer.

With the noteworthy exception of gender differences, the profile of the pray-er most likely to report having received answers to prayer requests is similar to the profile of those who engage in petitionary prayer (see Table 4 in chapter 2). Such persons are likely to be women, over age sixty-five, black, with less than a high school degree, and with an income under $15,000. Furthermore, they are likely to claim to be evangelical Christians (only 9 percent of the evangelicals but 30 percent of the non-evangelicals never had specific prayers answered) who regularly attend church services.

Although the petitionary prayer item was limited to material requests, it is reasonable to assume that persons who have the faith to pray for concrete needs will also pray for spiritual ones. (Data from the Akron Area Survey support this assertion. See Poloma and Pendleton, 1989; 1990; 1991.) Given the similar profiles of petitionary pray-ers and of those having prayers answered, it would appear that many who ask do receive that for which they have prayed. A modern and rational worldview may regard petitionary prayer as a form of magic, but it is a prayer form for which there are countless biblical examples. Most important for this discussion of religious experiences is the fact that unless people first asked, there could be no possible interactive experience of God responding to the petitions of those who pray.

Divine-Human Interaction through Inspiration

> As for you, the anointing you received from him remains in you, and you do not need anyone to teach you. But as his anointing teaches you about all things and as that anointing is real, not counterfeit—just as it has taught you, remain in him. (1 John 2:27)

The Gnostics of the early Christian church claimed to have a superior way of knowing faith mysteries through personal experiences. The institutional church responded to their excesses by challenging the validity of many religious experiences. Religious experiences are dangerous—especially if they challenge the theological pronouncements of the established religious order or if they divide believers into hostile camps. Yet, as we argued at the beginning of this chapter, the founders and prophets of great religions all had religious experiences which in some way challenged existing religious systems.

Contemporary main street mystics—those common folk who have experienced God in prayer—do not necessarily challenge theological formulations; perhaps they are even more likely to affirm basic Christian beliefs which have been handed down through the centuries. Evangelical Christians who have the experience of being "born-again" and charismatics who claim "Spirit baptism" often frame their experiences within orthodox theologies. They have come to *know* that which was previously unknown to them. Although our survey data do not permit us to sort out those who "challenge" from those who "affirm," we are able to consider the broader issue of being "taught" spiritual truths through prayer.

Margaret Poloma has done considerable research on the religious charismatic movement (Poloma, 1982; 1989), a Christian movement whose teachings include praying in tongues, belief in divine healing, prophecy miracles, and other seemingly miraculous happenings. During the course of collecting the data, Poloma heard countless examples of "Spirit baptism," an experience that allegedly opens the door to other charismatic phenomena reported in the early Christian church. The accounts, similar to the following given by a middle-aged pastor, tend to affirm a biblical orthodoxy:

> I began to really seek after God, trying to find what God had for me. I had heard about the baptism of the Holy

> Spirit just briefly on the radio. The man said that God
> wanted to baptize everyone in the Holy Spirit. I thought,
> "God, I want it—whatever it is." One day I stopped my
> car by a cornfield to get alone with God. I started to wor-
> ship him, and I was baptized right then. No help from
> anyone. It was just me and the Lord. (Poloma, 1989:46)

Although only a minority of Americans claim to be charismatic
Christians (approximately 12 to 13%), this experience does
demonstrate one way "spiritual truth" may be believed to be
taught through prayer experiences. Other experiences may be
less dramatic, and similar to this middle-aged woman's account:

> There are times I am left puzzled by a particular scripture
> verse. What I will do is ask the Holy Spirit to teach me
> what he wishes me to know about its meaning. I will ask
> him specifically how it can be applied to my life. When I
> receive the answer, I feel as if scales have been lifted from
> my eyes—as if the answer was there all along but I just
> didn't see it. (interview with author)

Relatively few of our respondents felt that God used
prayer to lead them into a deeper understanding of spiritual
truths. Only 12 percent of our respondents regularly had such
experiences. Women were somewhat more likely to report the
receiving of spiritual or biblical truths during prayer than were
men; 15 percent of the women as compared to 10 percent of
the men regularly have such experiences. Most other socio-
demographic variables were not statistically significant, including age, race, income, and education. As might be expected,
evangelical Christians or those who claimed to be born-again
were significantly more likely to experience divine interaction
in this way than were non-evangelicals; 23 percent of the
evangelicals but only 7 percent of non-evangelical pray-ers regularly had this experience. Believing God is teaching the prayer spiritual truths implies a still deeper level of intimacy than
the first three prayer experience items. Such prayer is more

than the pray-er talking to God; God's revelation of spiritual truths implies an intimate conversation in contrast to an impersonal monologue. It suggests a mutual presence that is akin to love or friendship, a mutual presence that is not regularly experienced by most people who pray.

Divine-Human Interaction through Participation in Action

I will instruct you and teach you the way you should go; I will counsel you and watch over you. (Ps. 32:8)

From the time of God's covenant with Abraham through the history of the founding of Christianity as reported in the book of Acts, God seemed to be giving specific instructions to men and women. Such divine leadings ranged from Abram being told to leave his country (Gen. 12:1), to Noah being given precise instructions for building the ark (Gen. 6–8), to Joseph being told in a dream to flee to Egypt with Mary and the child Jesus (Matt. 2:15), to Ananias being led to Paul shortly after Saul's conversion (Acts 9:11). In biblical accounts human beings were commonly regarded as capable of being participants in action with the Divine Actor.

Contemporary society in general, and social science in particular, take a dim view of such explicit divine guidance. History contains many accounts of those who have gone crazy and committed atrocious acts in the name of God. It is one thing to talk to God but quite another to experience him responding— especially if the response calls for specific directives. A slight majority of those who pray (57%), however, do claim to have been divinely inspired or "led by God" to perform some specific action. These survey data are unable to provide examples of such leadings, but accounts of them may be found in pious writings of varying sources. Such leadings may be as simple as having a sense to call a friend, only to find this friend is in some dire need, or as dramatic as Abram's call to leave his familiar land as God directed.

Guideposts, an inspirational magazine published by Ruth Stafford Peale and Norman Vincent Peale, frequently contains accounts of such divine leadings. A recent one by Christine Skillern, a seventy-year-old woman from Alabama, was an auto-biographical account of her experience of lying on a cold floor in her home after a fall. As she continued to pray for help through the night, she had an inspiration to begin to talk to a friend who lived some distance away. Skillern reported: "So I began calling, 'Roy, please come to me. I need you.' I said it aloud, over and over without stopping." Hours later she heard a knocking on the back door—it was Roy. The author continued:

> Roy and his wife were at home when he felt a strong urge to check on me. He told his wife, "I have to go to Chris-tine. Something has happened to her." When he knocked on my door, he got no answer, but something seemed to urge him. *Don't leave. Go to the back and knock again.* So he went around to the back door, knocked harder and finally heard me calling, "Come and help me. I need you." (Skillern, 1989:41)

Our survey data are unable to provide such colorful descriptions of divine leading, but what the data do reveal are those categories of persons most likely to experience divine guidance. As may be seen in the correlations presented in Table 2, age, sex, race, and education are all related to having reported being "led by God." Those who have *never* had this religious experience are more likely to be male (42% of the men versus 35% of the women never experienced such divine guidance), under 29 years of age (52% as compared with 26% of respondents over age 65), and high school or college graduates (31% of those with less than a high school degree versus 43% of those with a high school diploma or more education). Non-evangelicals are con-siderably more likely to report *never* having experienced divine guidance than are evangelicals (48% versus 20%), with evangelicals also being significantly more likely to report regular experiences of being "led by God" (15%). Black respondents are more likely to *regularly* encounter God in this way than are whites (19% versus 8%).

These five religious experiences, while only representative of the range available to pray-ers, do appear to represent different degrees of interaction with God during prayer. Since they share the common denominator of being prayer experiences, it is not surprising that statistical analysis permits us to treat them as a scale.[3] Combining them into a single index will enable us to more accurately profile those most likely to have religious experiences, to relate these experiences to the types of prayer delineated in the previous chapter, and to begin analyzing the effects of such experiences.

REFINING THE DESCRIPTION

Using a single item to approximate the classes of religious experience identified by Stark can be misleading. Questions may not always be understood by respondents as they are intended by the questioner. For this reason, basing a conclusion on the responses to a single item question may not be entirely accurate. As a further check on the analysis presented on the individual prayer experiences, the five items were combined to form an index. Those respondents with 15 to 20 points on this index were labeled as "high" experiencers (n = 256); those with 11 to 14 points, as "medium" (n = 229); and those with less than 11 points, as "low" on religious experience (n = 259).

As may be seen in the last line of Table 2 and in detail in Table 3, some of the demographic items that were related to single measures of prayer experience are no longer statistically significant. Income, race, and education do not correlate with the degree to which a pray-er may be described as high or low

3. Cronbach's alpha for these five prayer experience items is .87.

TABLE 3
Prayer Experiences by Select Variables*

	Low	Medium	High
Sex			
Men	41%	30%	29%
Women	29%	32%	39%
Age			
18–24	29%	39%	32%
25–29	49%	25%	26%
30–49	38%	30%	32%
50–64	31%	35%	35%
65 or older	26%	30%	44%
Born-again			
Evangelical	14%	30%	56%
Non-evangelical	46%	31%	23%
Denomination			
Protestant	29%	31%	40%
Catholic	40%	33%	26%

NOTE: Income, race, and education were not statistically related to the prayer experience scale.

*Percentages may add up to more than 100% due to rounding.

on religious prayer experiences. Sex ($r = .13$) and age ($r = .11$) are the only two socio-demographic variables to be related to private prayer experiences. Men are significantly less likely than women and younger persons are somewhat less likely than those over age 65 to earn a high score on this scale.

The strongest predictor of a high score on the prayer experience scale is whether or not a person accepts the designation of being "born-again" (r = .37). People were asked, "Would you describe yourself as a born-again Christian?" Forty-four percent of the Protestant respondents (n = 586) and 11 percent of the Catholics (n = 259) responded affirmatively. It is not surprising that relatively few Catholics consider themselves to be born-again, a self-designation that is Protestant in origin. What was surprising is that Catholics, whose religion is often regarded by scholars to be more "mystical" than the more rationally oriented Protestantism, did score significantly lower on prayer experiences. Looking more closely at these differences, however, it appears that non-evangelical Protestants (those who do not regard themselves as twice born) resemble Catholics in their being lower in prayer experiences than evangelicals. The positive relationship between being Protestant and having prayer experiences is due largely to the evangelical Protestants having more prayer experiences than mainstream Protestants.

Bivariate analyses such as those we have been presenting are very informative and descriptive, but the results may be overly simplistic. It is possible, for example, that the reason women are more likely to have prayer experiences is not due to gender differences but rather to the fact that women respondents are more likely to be older. It may thus be that age—not sex—is really related to experiences during prayer. Using a statistical procedure known as multiple regression analysis, we were able to take a closer look at the effects of select variables on prayer experiences.

We entered sex, race, income, education, and age (in addition to whether the respondent claimed to be born-again) as independent variables into a single equation. The strongest correlate with prayer experience is whether or not the respondent is a born-again (evangelical) Christian. The profile of a person who scores high on the prayer experience scale continues to be an evangelical, older female. Put another way, evangelicals, women, and older persons continue to be more likely to have intense prayer experiences than non-evangelicals, men, and younger persons.

DO PRAYER EXPERIENCES
MAKE A DIFFERENCE?

In writing about religious experiences, theologian Denis Edwards (1983:6) compares the nature of human experiences to that of religious ones. After raising the question of what it means when we say that we have some experience of another human person, Edwards replies: "Usually we mean (1) that we have had one or more encounters with the person, and (2) that we have formed some kind of interpretation or understanding of this person as a result of these encounters." In other words, there is an encounter, and that encounter results in some kind of interpretation.

Most pray-ers believe they have encountered God—through a deep sense of God's presence, through answered prayer, through a sense of divine inspiration and guidance. Do such experiences affect the pray-er's understanding of God? In Chapter 2 we considered how the types of prayer were related to feeling a sense of closeness to God. As a final analysis for Chapter 3, we will again look at the respondents' self-evaluation of their intimacy with God. The first step in the analysis will consider the relationship between prayer experiences and the four types of prayer we identified in the last chapter. Next we will view the prayer experience scores in light of perceived distance from or closeness to God. Finally we will analyze the relative importance of the four prayer types and prayer experiences for the respondents' perceptions of intimacy with the Divine.

Prayer Experiences and
Types of Prayer

All four types of prayer correlate with religious experiences during prayer, although some demonstrate stronger rela-

---

TABLE 4
Relationship between Prayer Experience Scores
and Prayer Types

Types of Prayer°	Prayer Experience Scores		
	Low	Medium	High
Meditative	13%	32%	56%
Colloquial	26%	34%	40%
Ritual	27%	27%	40%
Petitionary	25%	27%	48%

Pearson's r: Meditative = .51
Colloquial = .36
Ritual = .12
Petitionary = .26

°Based only on high scores for prayer types; i.e., those who engaged in all of the items included in each scale.

---

tionships than do others. As may be seen in Table 4, only 13 percent of those who practice meditative prayer had low scores on the prayer experience scale. Approximately one-fourth of those who utilized the other prayer forms scored low on prayer experiences. Meditative prayer clearly showed the strongest relationship to experiencing God in prayer; it was followed by colloquial prayer, petitionary prayer, and ritual prayer.[4]

Since most pray-ers engage in more than one prayer form, it is helpful to use multiple regression analysis to determine

4. The bivariate correlations between types of prayer and prayer experiences are as follows: meditative, r = .51; colloquial, r = .36; petitionary, r = .26; and ritual, r = .12. This ordering holds when a single multiple regression equation is run, with betas of .31 (meditative prayer), .20 (colloquial prayer), and .11 (petitionary). (Ritual prayer was not statistically significant in the multiple regression equation.)

which of the types of prayer is most likely to produce religious experiences. The results of such testing provide even stronger support for the findings suggested in the bivariate analyses. Although the more active forms of colloquial and petitionary prayer also demonstrate relationships to religious experience, those who employ the more passive form of meditative prayer are clearly the most likely to perceive that they frequently encounter God in prayer.

Prayer Experiences and
Perceived Closeness to God

As one might expect, there is a relatively strong relationship between experiencing God in prayer and perceived closeness to God. As may be seen in Table 5, 80 percent of those who were low on the prayer experience scale rated their relationship to God as being "distant." In contrast, only 13 percent of those who felt very close to God were low on prayer experiences. Looking only at this relationship and those just presented in the previous section for different types of prayer, it remains unclear whether the use of a prayer form or a claiming of prayer experience is the better predictor of a close relationship with God.

Prayer Types, Prayer Experiences, and
Relationship to God

So far our analysis has demonstrated that the four prayer types are all related to perceived closeness to God (see the results presented in Chapter 2). So, too, are prayer experience scores. Use of multiple regression analysis once again will enable us to determine whether prayer experiences and/or one or more of the four prayer types helps to best account for perceptions of intimacy with God. The findings are in line with the results we have presented thus far.

As expected, pray-ers who scored high on religious experi-

TABLE 5
Relationship between Prayer Experience Scale
and Closeness to God

Closeness to God	Prayer Experience Score		
	Low	Medium	High
Distant	80%	15%	5%
Intermediate	40%	37%	23%
Close	13%	31%	56%
(Pearson's r = .50)			

ences were most likely to feel very close to God.[5] In other words, those who responded affirmatively to the five questions tapping prayer experiences were the most likely to select a 6 or 7, indicating a very close relationship with God. Three of the four prayer types—ritual, colloquial, and meditative—also demonstrated statistically significant relationships to the respondent's perceptions of intimacy with God. Only petitionary prayer was not statistically significant in this regression equation. We also sought to determine whether participation in church ritual and the experience of being born-again were better predictors of a sense of closeness to God than were prayer experiences. Church attendance and the identification of a respondent as an evangelical Christian were related to this sense of divine intimacy, but these partial correlations were much weaker than the one for religious experiences. These data suggest that while some select religiosity measures, including

5. The R Square for the equation regressing perceived closeness to God on the four types of prayer and prayer experiences is .35. The beta values are as follows: prayer experiences = .39; meditative prayer = .19; colloquial prayer = .10; ritual prayer = .09; and petitionary prayer = .01 (n.s.).

three of the four prayer forms, show a clear relationship to feeling close to God, it is religious experience during prayer that is the best indicator of such divine intimacy.[6]

SUMMARY AND CONCLUSIONS

Religious experiences are commonplace. Although relatively few persons may hear voices and see visions, most pray-ers do perceive that they have encountered God. These experiences range from simply noting the presence of God to being aware of the mutual presence and an affective relationship, to being a fellow participant in the action of God. Those who report the whole range of religious experiences identified in this survey are also the most likely to perceive that they have a very close and intimate relationship with God.

Based on the data presented in this chapter we can state with some confidence that Americans are not only having religious experiences but that these experiences are at the heart of their relationship with God. Religious ritual and belief may commonly accompany or precede these experiences, but the experiences themselves may be regarded as the vital link between pray-ers and the God to whom they pray.

Some readers may deprecate such findings, asserting that religious experiences and subjective perceptions of closeness to God are merely byproducts of a narcissistic culture. These more mystical pray-ers may be heavenly, but are they of any earthly good? Having demonstrated that prayer takes different forms and that religious experiences appear to accompany some forms more than others, we will now turn to some of the effects

6. Even when demographic control variables are in place, religious experience is by far the strongest correlate of intimacy with the Divine. Having less education (beta = .07), being black (beta = .07), being female (beta = .07), and being older (beta = .06) do show statistically weak partial correlations with the pray-er's perception of being close to God. The category of prayer experiences (beta = .33) retained its strong positive relationship with perceptions of divine intimacy.

of prayer and prayer experiences. The next chapter will explore the relationship between two seemingly disparate practices: prayer and political action.

WORKS CITED

Bloom, Metropolitan Anthony
  1975   *Living Prayer*. Springfield, Ill.: Templegate.
Edwards, Denis
  1983   *Human Experience of God*. New York: Paulist Press.
Emerging Trends
  1985   Prayer in American Life. Vol. 7, no. 3 (March). Princeton, N.J.: Princeton Research Center.
Maslow, Abraham H.
  1964   *Religions, Values, and Peak-Experiences*. New York: Viking Press.
Poloma, Margaret M.
  1982   *The Charismatic Movement: Is There a New Pentecost?* Boston: Twayne Publishers.
  1989   *The Assemblies of God at the Crossroads: Charisma and Institutional Dilemmas*. Knoxville: University of Tennessee Press.
Poloma, Margaret M., and Brian F. Pendleton
  1989   Exploring Types of Prayer and the Quality of Life. *Review of Religious Research* (September):46–53.
  1990   Religious Domains and General Well-Being. *Social Indicators* (Spring):255–76.
  1991   The Effects of Prayer and Prayer Experiences on General Well-Being. *Journal of Psychology and Theology* 19(1):71–83.
Skillern, Christine
  1989   Call Roy Stanley. *Guideposts* (November):40–41.
Spilka, Bernard, Ralph W. Hood, Jr., and Richard L. Gorsuch
  1985   *The Psychology of Religion: An Empirical Approach*. Englewood Cliffs, N.J.: Prentice-Hall.
Stark, Rodney
  1965   A Taxonomy of Religious Experience. *Journal for the Scientific Study of Religion* 5:97–116.

4

DO PRAYER AND
POLITICS MIX?
Personal Prayer and Political Activism

> Politics and the pulpit are terms that have little agreement. No sound ought to be heard in the church but the healing voice of Christian charity.
>
> Edmund Burke, 1790,
> *Reflecting on Revolutions in France*

The interface of religion and politics has been a cause for concern and conflict since the advent of society. From ancient theocracies to postmodern secular governments, the kingdoms of God and humankind have been often locked in struggle. Beginning with developments in the American colonies, the United States has its own somewhat unique history of the tensions between the two kingdoms. Largely people who had emigrated for a variety of strong religious reasons, the founders of the United States tended to regard religion differently from their contemporary European revolutionaries, who considered religion the enemy of political change. The result of this early predisposition has been not only a relatively high mutual tolerance among the different religious groups in this country, but a widespread belief in the positive social value of church going and religious activities.

Paradoxically, however, there has also been what Thomas Jefferson metaphorically referred to as a "wall" between church and state. As sociologist Robert Bellah and his colleagues (Bellah et al., 1985:219–20) have noted, this so-called separation of church and state was not a vision of the early colonists. America had a religious meaning from the very beginning, with the early settlers seeking "religious freedom, not as we would conceive of it today, but rather [as an] escape from a religious establishment with which they disagreed in order to found a new established church." The authors of the best-selling *Habits of the Heart* summarize the historical transition from the tight linkage of religion and public life to the increasingly pluralistic mosaic we have come to take for granted in America as follows:

> It was undoubtedly pressure from the dissenting sects, with their large popular following, on the one hand, and from that significant portion of the educated and politically effective elite influenced by Enlightenment thought on the other, that finally led to the disestablishment of religion in the United States. Yet the full implications of disestablishment were not felt immediately. In the early decades of the republic, American society, particularly in small towns, remained stable and hierarchical, and religion continued to play its unifying public role. (Bellah et al., 1985:221–22)

In other words, in early American society religion was "public and unified"; in contemporary America it is "private and diverse." Religion has been increasingly individualized and privatized, although at the same time it has continued to be allowed some public functions.

The process of privatizing religion has been accompanied by a noticeable strain "between the withdrawal of religion into purely private spirituality and the biblical imperative to see religion be involved with the whole of life" (Bellah et al., 1985:248). This tension may be seen in the general development of the so-called Christian Right (Rothenberg and Newport, 1984; Liebman and Wuthnow, 1983), a conservative blend of politics and religion that has made its presence felt in the 1980s—a presence that is certain to be carried into the new decade. Many religious groups are no longer satisfied with admonishing their followers to lead good and holy lives; they at times insist on the need for direct political involvement. This is evidenced particularly in the fight to make abortion illegal in this country, a battle that has already included the destruction of property and a flagrant disregard for civil liberties, and conceivably could escalate into violent confrontations between opposing groups.

It is perhaps because of just such potential for conflict that American folk wisdom admonishes against the mingling of religion and politics. This prohibition is reinforced by an ethos which insists that religion and religious organizations should stay out of politics—a point of view about which questions were asked in this Gallup survey. When asked, "Should the churches keep out of political matters, or should they express their views on day-to-day social and political questions?" a clear majority (60%) of those who offered an opinion said churches should "keep out." Respondents were also asked whether they agreed or disagreed with the following statement: "Religious organizations should persuade senators and representatives to enact legislation on ethical and moral issues they would like to see become law." Once again a clear majority of those who expressed an opinion (60%) disagreed with the prospect of religious organizations becoming politically involved—even when, as the statement indicates, the issues are "ethical" and "moral." What these data suggest is that while the ethos of a separation of religion and politics is still in place, we are a divided people. A significant minority of respondents who expressed an opinion on both of these attitude questions (40%) felt that the church and religious organizations *should* get involved in the political arena.

What we will do in this chapter is to describe briefly the interface of religiosity, political attitudes, and religiously motivated political action. We will then consider whether prayer—a measure of religiosity that reflects the private sphere—plays any role in accounting for public political activities.

CHURCHES AND POLITICS: PUBLIC ATTITUDES

The majority of the respondents were negatively disposed to the Gallup questions measuring attitudes toward church involvement in political matters. Only a minority of the respondents (40%) felt that churches should express their views on social and political questions. Similarly only 40 percent felt that religious organizations should work for legislative changes on ethical and moral issues. A majority expressed negative attitudes toward church intervention in the political arena, whether this involvement be in word or deed.

As may be seen in Table 1, standard demographic factors of race, education, income, age, and sex for the most part were not correlated with differences of opinion. (Only education and age demonstrate weak correlations with the view that churches should express views on political issues, with lesser educated and older persons more likely to favor church involvement.)

The correlations in Table 1 present in summary form the relationships that may be observed between attitudes toward church intervention in politics and personal religiosity, prayer, and demographic measures. A descriptive presentation of the percentages behind some of these correlations may be found in Table 2.

The religiosity measures included in Table 2 were all related positively with a favorable attitude toward the mixing of

TABLE 1
Attitudes toward Church Involvement in Politics
(Select Bivariate Relations)

Churches should express their views on day-to-day social and political questions. (40% = agree)

Demographics

Race	ns
Education	-.08°
Income	ns
Age	.09°
Sex	ns

General Religiosity Measures

Religion is very important	.20°°°
Church member	.16°°°
Attended church last Sunday	.19°°°
Evangelical Christian	.18°°°
Closeness to God	.11°°

Prayer Measures

Ever prays	.12°°
Colloquial prayer	.11°°
Ritual prayer	ns
Petitionary prayer	.10°°
Meditative prayer	.17°°°
Prayer experiences	.20°°°

Religious organizations should work for legislative changes on ethical and moral issues. (40% = agree)

Demographics

Race	ns
Education	ns
Income	ns
Age	ns
Sex	ns

General Religiosity Measures

Religion is very important	.29°°°
Church member	.22°°°
Attended church last Sunday	.28°°°

(*Continued on page 72*)

TABLE 1 (*Continued*)

General Religiosity Measures

Evangelical Christian	.27°°°
Closeness to God	.22°°°

Prayer measures

Ever pray	.16°°°
Colloquial prayer	.11°
Ritual Prayer	ns
Petitionary prayer	.18°°°
Meditative prayer	.17°°°
Prayer experiences	.28°°°

Significance levels = °p = .05; °°p = .01; °°°p = .001

ns = not significant

TABLE 2
Should the churches keep out of political matters, or should they express their views on day-to-day social and political questions?

	Express Views	Keep Out
Importance of religion in life°		
Very important	48%	53%
Fairly important	37%	63%
Not very important	19%	82%
Church member°		
Yes	46%	54%
No	28%	72%
Born-again Christian°		
Yes	54%	47%
No	34%	66%

TABLE 2 (*Continued*)

	Express Views	Keep Out
Respondent prays°		
Yes	43%	57%
No	23%	77%
Type of Prayer		
Meditational°		
High	51%	49%
Low	35%	66%
Colloquial		
High	43%	57%
Low	39%	62%
Ritual		
High	41%	60%
Low	43%	57%
Petitionary°		
High	49%	51%
Low	38%	62%
Prayer Experiences°		
High	57%	44%
Medium	42%	58%
Low	32%	68%

°Chi Square for cross tabulation is significant at the .001 level or lower; other items are not statistically significant.

religion and politics. For example, only 19 percent of those for whom religion is *not* very important in life felt that the churches should express political views, while 48 percent of those for whom religion was very important supported such action. This same pattern was found for church members, with 54 percent of members but 72 percent of nonmembers asserting that churches should stay out of politics. The sociological profile of a person who is likely to support the right of churches to express their views on day-to-day social and political questions and to feel that religious organizations should work for legislative changes on ethical and moral issues is as follows: a person for whom religion is very important, a church member who attended church the Sunday before this survey was conducted, someone who feels very close to God, and one who is likely to identify as a born-again Christian. This person is one who practices frequent prayer and makes use of colloquial, petitionary, and meditative forms of prayer, but is less likely to engage in ritual prayer.

Describing the differences between those for whom religion is salient and those who are less religious presents only part of the story. It should be noted that religiously oriented respondents are nearly evenly divided in their political opinions. This split in opinion is reflected in the figures presented in Table 2. For example, of those who regarded religion as "very important" for their lives, 48 percent felt that churches should express their views on day-to-day social and political questions, while 53 percent felt they should not. Similarly 47 percent of those who claimed to be born-again Christians believed that churches should stay out of politics, as compared with 54 percent who felt that churches should express their views. While those who score higher on religious dimensions are much more likely to favor church involvement, there is a nearly even split among the self-identified evangelicals. (For a discussion of a similar pattern among Assemblies of God adherents, see Poloma, 1987; 1989.)

Although this nearly even split in opinion may be seen in the correlations and cross tabulations for most religiosity items and political attitudes, one prayer measure does demonstrate a somewhat stronger relationship to the approval of church involvement in politics than do the other religiosity measures. As may be seen from the correlations reported in Table 1 and the descriptive percentages in Table 2, those who have more regular experiences of God during prayer are more likely to approve of the involvement of religious groups in political affairs. While only 44 percent of those who experienced God speaking, answering prayer, and guiding their actions felt churches should not express their views on political issues, 57 percent who scored high on religious experiences felt that such action was appropriate.

The simple bivariate analysis employing only two variables at a time was extended to a multivariate analysis to determine whether the private or the public measures of religiosity were more important in predicting positive attitudes toward church involvement in politics. Using multiple regression analysis, we tested first the relationship between religiosity and attitudes toward the expression of political views by churches. The same thing was done with the question about religious organizations working for legislative changes. These two questions were "regressed" against church membership and attendance, subjective measures of religiosity, and prayer items. The results indicate that prayer experiences is the single most important factor in accounting for a pro-church involvement stance.[1] In other words, those who regularly experience God in prayer are the most likely persons to favor church involvement in politics, whether or not they consider themselves to be evangelicals, attend church regularly, use a particular form of prayer, or profess religious salience.

Our analysis thus far points to two important facts. First, it suggests that standard demographic factors are less likely to be

1. The question inquiring about religious organizations working for legislative changes was regressed against church membership, evangelical identification, church attendance, religious salience, the four types of prayer, and prayer experiences. The R Square for this multiple regression equation was .15, with significant betas for prayer experience (.15), evangelical status (.14), and church attendance (.10).

When the question inquiring about the appropriateness of churches expressing their views on political questions was regressed against these same variables, the R Square was .08. Only the beta for prayer experiences (.15) was statistically significant at the .001 level.

predictors of a supportive attitude toward the mixing of politics and religion than are religious factors. Those who are more religious, whether the measures are public ones of church affiliation and involvement or the private ones dealing with personal prayer, are more likely to approve of churches being involved in political action. Second, it appears that privatized religiosity as measured by our prayer experiences is a leading factor in predicting a positive attitude toward mixing politics and religion—even more important than public religious acts, self-identification as an evangelical, or church membership.

While people may express opinions on issues, there is often a disjuncture between what people *say* and what they *do*—in this case between verbally supporting church involvement in politics and actually becoming involved in them. Some religious respondents seem to favor political activities by the churches, but are they more likely than others to become involved in specific political action? This is an issue to which we will now turn.

RELIGIOUSLY MOTIVATED POLITICAL ACTIVITY

In order to address the issue of political action that stemmed from religious commitment, respondents were asked the following question: "During the last three years have you done any of the following things largely because of your own religious beliefs?" and were given the following choices:

> prayed in support of a particular issue or candidate
> voted for a particular political candidate
> talked to people about why they should vote for one of the candidates
> written a letter to the editor about a national problem

made a contribution to a candidate or a political organization
attended any political meetings or rallies
worked for a particular political candidate
demonstrated or protested about a national problem
joined an organization to deal with a national problem.

Only one in four respondents was religiously motivated to engage in the two most popular activities—praying (27%) and voting for a particular candidate (25%). Despite the support many showed for political activism by their churches, individuals were much less likely to engage in political activities. Only 10 percent wrote a letter to the editor about a national problem, 8 percent attended a political meeting, and 5 percent demonstrated for or against a national problem. A summary of these findings may be found in Table 3.

The categorizing of the political activities in Table 3 as "candidate/issues" and "national problems" reflects the results of factor analysis, a statistical procedure which allowed us to determine the two major common denominators underlying the nine issues about political activities and to consolidate further analysis.[2] These two major categories were (1) political activity that may be locally oriented toward the support of particular candidates and issues, and (2) political involvement that focused on national problems. Both categories were considered separately with a special interest given to the role prayer may play in such involvement. The results of the bivariate analysis may be found in the correlations presented in Table 4.

Although few of the demographic variables were found to be statistically related to political action, most of the religious variables did demonstrate statistically significant correlations.

2. The items that clustered on the two factors were then submitted to a reliability check. The candidate/issues questions produced a Cronbach's alpha of .63; Cronbach's alpha for the national problems questions was .43.

TABLE 3
Political Involvement

During the last three years have you done any of the following largely because of your own religious beliefs?

	Yes
Candidate/Issues	
Voted for a particular political candidate	25%
Talked to people about why they should vote for one of the candidates	18%
Worked for a particular political candidate	6%
Made a contribution to a candidate or political organization	10%
Attended any political meetings or rallies	8%
Prayed in support of a particular issue or candidate	27%
National Problems	
Written a letter to the editor about a national problem	10%
Joined an organization to deal with a national problem	6%
Demonstrated or protested about a national problem	5%

Persons who were more religious not only were likely to pray for a particular candidate or issue, they also were more likely to vote, talk to people about politics, make contributions to political campaigns, attend political rallies, and work for political candidates.

Of particular interest to us is the role that prayer plays in political activities. The data suggest that one of the fruits of prayer is a heightened political awareness that lessens the separation between the private religious side and the public political side of life. Those who prayed were more likely to be involved in political activities that were candidate/issue

TABLE 4
Correlations between Politics Scales
and Select Variables

	Candidate/Issues	National Problems
Demographics		
Race	ns	ns
Education	ns	.10
Income	ns	ns
Age	-.10	ns
Sex	ns	ns
General Religiosity Measures		
Importance of religion	.27	.12
Church member	.20	.11
Church attendance	.23	.09
Evangelical Christian	.24	.11
Feeling close to God	.24	.11
Protestant/Catholic	ns	ns
Prayer Measures		
Ever pray	.16	ns
Colloquial prayer	.15	ns
Ritual prayer	.18	ns
Petitionary prayer	.16	ns
Meditative prayer	.22	ns
Prayer experiences	.29	.11

NOTE: All reported correlations are statistically significant at a probability level of .01 or less.

ns = not significant

oriented. Even stronger relationships may be found for those who engage in meditative prayer and have more intense religious experiences and political activity, particularly that which is candidate/issue oriented.

The relationship between political participation and prayer experiences may be easier to see in the percentages presented in Table 5. Only 25 percent of the total sample claimed to vote for a particular candidate because of personal religious beliefs. Of the minority who did so, 45 percent scored high in religious experiences. Correspondingly, only 21 percent of those who voted had no or only one such experience. This same pattern may be seen in all of the single items as well as in the two composite political activities scales derived from these items. A total of 18 percent of the total sample scored high on the issue/candidate political scale (i.e., they were involved in at least two of the six activities). Of those persons, 56 percent scored high on prayer experiences, while 15 percent scored low. In other words, the "mystics" who in some way experience God in prayer are more politically active than those who have fewer prayer experiences.

The story of Martha and Mary comes to mind (Luke 10:38-42). The tension between Martha, who was busily preparing dinner for Jesus, and her sister Mary, who meanwhile sat at Jesus' feet, is often used as a springboard for discussing the merits of action versus contemplation. Perhaps because Jesus commended Mary for "having chosen the better part," some have assumed that "doing" and "praying" are uneasy partners and put primary emphasis on one or the other. These data suggest that for the minority who are involved in some forms of political activity, praying is a strong correlate of action. Although whether or not a person prays demonstrates a moderate relationship to the candidate/issue scale ($r = .16$), the intensity of prayer experiences shows a much stronger relationship ($r = .29$). Those who are involved in meditative prayer,

TABLE 5
Prayer Experience by Political Participation

Issue/Candidate Items	Total Sample (n = 1,030)	Prayer Experiences*		
		Low	Medium	High
Voted for	25%	21%	34%	45%
Worked for	6%	12%	29%	59%
Talked about	18%	21%	28%	50%
Made contributions	10%	15%	28%	57%
Attended meeting	8%	18%	16%	66%
Prayed for	27%	14%	29%	58%
*Combined Index***				
Low	56%	44%	32%	24%
Medium	26%	27%	31%	42%
High	18%	15%	29%	56%
National Problems Items				
Wrote letter	10%	19%	29%	53%
Joined organization	6%	18%	33%	49%
Demonstrated	5%	28%	40%	32%
Combined Index				
Low	88%	36%	31%	33%
High	12%	20%	32%	48%

*Low designation indicates less than two prayer experiences; medium, two or three prayer experiences; high, four or five experiences.

** Low designation for the Issue/candidate index indicates no political activity; medium indicates involvement in one activity; high indicates more than one activity. Low designation for the National Problems index represents no activity; high, one or more activities.

n = sample size

persons who, as we have demonstrated in Chapter 3, Table 4, are much more likely to have intense religious experiences, are also more likely to be politically active. It does not appear to be a case for Martha *or* Mary, but rather one for Martha *and* Mary!

The same pattern, although not as strong, may be seen in the relationship between prayer and national political action. Very few persons were involved in writing letters to editors, joining organizations, or demonstrating about national problems. For the most part, pray-ers were no more likely to be involved in these activities than were nonpray-ers. As may be seen from the correlations presented in Table 4, neither the incidence of personal prayer nor the type of prayer employed appears to be related to becoming involved in political activities that bear on national problems. The intensity of prayer experience, however, does show a positive correlation with writing a letter to the editor and joining an organization to deal with a national problem. (The few respondents who demonstrated about a national problem could not be differentiated by their responses to any of the prayer items, including prayer experience.)

When the three items are combined to form a national problems index, prayer experience continues to be an important indicator of an activist stance. Twelve percent of the total sample scored high on the national problems index. Of these persons, only 20 percent were low on religious experiences, with the remainder having two or more encounters with God during prayer. Although fewer persons are involved in national political action than with local issues and candidates, highly religious persons are more likely to be involved. In fact, the persons who may be called "mystics"—the ones who sense, feel, and hear from God during prayer—are the most likely to engage in political action with religious motivation.[3]

3. The importance of prayer experiences for predicting political activism persisted when the data were analyzed using multiple regression procedures. When the

SUMMARY AND CONCLUSIONS

Although a wall between religion and politics is often regarded as desirable, our data suggest that this wall is more permeable than some might like. Many religiously oriented persons are favorably disposed, at least under some circumstances, toward the integration of politics and religion. Perhaps even more interesting is the finding that the best religious indicator of a strong supportive stance for the mixing of politics and religion is a private measure of religiosity—the experience of God during prayer.

Although far fewer persons become involved in political activities than have opinions on political matters, many of these people are religiously motivated. Once again, however, prayer experience proves to be the best predictor of political activism. In other words, those who have a highly developed privatized spirituality, whether or not they are involved in public forms of religiosity, are the most likely to favor church involvement in politics and to become politically active themselves. What are we to make of this?

Those who experience communion with God in prayer undoubtedly perceive they have a strong ally. God is not someone who is "up there in the sky" but someone who walks and talks with these pray-ers. Some, albeit a minority, may feel that God is leading them to become involved in the nitty-gritty world of politics and protest. Such persons, acting on the basis of their convictions, may have a stronger motivation to carry out their perceived political duties than do those who are not religiously motivated. It is not simply that religious form dictates

---

candidate/issues scale was regressed against church membership, evangelical status, church attendance, religious salience, types of prayer, and prayer experiences, 12 percent of the variance was explained. Only the beta for prayer experiences (.17) was statistically significant.

Religious variables were able to explain only 5 percent of the variance for the issues political activism scale. Once again, however, only the beta for prayer experiences (.20) was statistically significant.

such involvement but rather that religious experiences appear to be a driving force.

Despite the quotation by Edmund Burke used to open this chapter, politics and pulpit do mix for many people. This is most evident not through looking at a public religious form but rather in analyzing private religious experiences that cause some pray-ers to believe they are in collaboration with God.

Burke's quotation reminds us of yet another function—undoubtedly the most important—of religion, namely, that of charity or love. In a famous line from *An Essay on Criticism*, satirist Alexander Pope writes: "To err is human, to forgive divine." Forgiveness is often imputed to be a godlike quality, a reflection of a loving deity. What is the relationship (if any) between communion with the divinity in prayer and the ability to forgive? This is an issue that we will explore in Chapter 5.

WORKS CITED

Bellah, Robert N., Richard Madsen, William M. Sullivan, Ann Swidler, and Steven M. Tipton
   1985   *Habits of the Heart*. New York: Harper & Row.
Liebman, Robert C., and Robert Wuthnow
   1983   *The New Christian Right*. New York: Aldine Publishing Company.
Poloma, Margaret M.
   1987   Pentecostals and Politics in North and Central America. In *Prophetic Religions and Politics*, edited by Jeffrey K. Hadden and Anson Shupe. New York: Paragon House.
   1989   *The Assemblies of God at the Crossroads*. Knoxville: University of Tennessee Press.
Rothenberg, Stuart, and Frank Newport
   1984   *The Evangelical Voter*. Washington, D.C.: The Institute for Government and Politics of the Free Congress Research and Education Foundation.

5

UNLESS YOU
FORGIVE OTHERS:
Prayer and Forgiveness

> Write the wrongs that are done to you in sand, but write the
> good things that happen to you on a piece of marble. Let go of
> all emotions, such as resentment and retaliation, which dimin-
> ish you, and hold onto the emotions, such as gratitude and joy,
> which increase you.
>
> — Arab proverb

Forgiveness is a part of proverbial wisdom that is deeply
embedded in our Judeo-Christian culture. It is encouraged by
writers who promote folk sayings as well as by theologians and
spiritual writers. Despite its significance, forgiveness, as Dr. E.
Mansell Pattison (1965) pointed out more than twenty-five
years ago, is a concept that "has primarily been of theologic concern, regarded as alien to psychotherapy." It remains a
phenomenon that is embedded in our common-sense worldview but one on which little empirical information is available.

In 1984 Morton Kaufman noted that although forgiveness
plays "an integral part in the progress toward maturity induced
by the curative process of psychotherapy," the concept has
"found virtually no place in the psychological literature." In an

article published three years later, Donald Hope (1987:240) made a related observation: "The process of forgiveness is a key part of the psychological healing process, but . . . it is rarely recognized as such." Instead it is "intuitively" practiced by talented psychotherapists as they teach clients to "work through," "let go," or "accept" the hurts of the past.

The therapist who was seeking deeper understanding of the nature and process of forgiveness would have found little guidance from professional journals. In the mid-1980s neither the term *forgiveness* nor its synonyms were indexed in *Psychological Abstracts*, the *Comprehensive Textbook of Psychiatry*, or the *Handbook of Family Therapy* (Hope, 1987). This problem has been recently rectified, in part through the publication of more articles on the topic and also through the inclusion of the term "forgiveness" as one researched by *Psychological Abstracts*.

A recent search through *Psychological Abstracts* produced fifty-six references that touch at least in some small way on the issue of forgiveness or self-forgiveness. Many of these articles appeared in two Christian psychology journals, demonstrating the impact Christian professionals have had in alerting behavioral scientists to their earlier oversight. Other articles appearing primarily in counseling journals use case studies to illustrate the importance of forgiveness for mental health. Only four of the articles (roughly 7%) included survey, interview, or experimental data that went beyond the reporting of a few illustrative situations or case reports.[1]

1. The four pioneering studies on forgiveness are diverse in their focus and methods. An experiment by Roloff and Janiszewski (1989) with 120 undergraduates in part explored the relationship between intimacy and communicated forgiveness. Another set of studies by Enright, Santos, and Al-Mabuk (1989) tested a cognitive developmental model of forgiveness and reported that people's understanding of forgiveness developed with age. Rosenzweig-Smith (1988) presented data from a study of thirty-one adult adoptees which related forgiveness to a successful mother-child reunion. In a study of 221 kindergarten and school-age children, Darby and Schlenker (1982) found a relationship between types of apologies rendered and forgiveness of high- and low-responsibility transgressions.

The few empirical studies, the counseling reports, and the theoretical literature on the relevance and processes of forgiveness (cf. Parsons, 1988; Bonar, 1989; Pingleton, 1989; Shontz and Rosenak, 1988; Ritzman, 1987; Fitzgibbons, 1986; Brink, 1985) point to the important part forgiveness plays in the psychological healing process. Fitzgibbons, for example, in urging therapists to use forgiveness in the treatment of anger noted:

> Forgiveness is a powerful therapeutic intervention which frees people from their anger and from the guilt which is often a result of unconscious anger. Forgiveness (1) helps individuals forget the painful experiences of their past and frees them from the subtle control of individuals and events of the past; (2) facilitates the reconciliation of relationships more than the expression of anger; and (3) decreases the likelihood that anger will be misdirected in later loving relationships and lessens the fear of being punished because of unconscious violent impulses. (Fitzgibbons, 1986:630)

He concludes his argument by asserting that "mental health professionals are in a unique and significant position to help individuals relinquish their anger without inflicting harm on others through the use of forgiveness" (p. 634).

Although discussions on the importance of forgiveness are becoming more common in clinical journals, they still suffer from a lack of empirical data—particularly data from which generalizations may be made to a nonclinical population. We know little from empirical research about how people feel about forgiveness (e.g., whether they regard it as appropriate behavior) or whether a spirit of forgiveness has an effect on a person's life. Social scientists have shown even less interest in researching the topic than have their cousins in the behavioral sciences.

Recognizing that the social and behavioral sciences have ignored this important topic, George Gallup included a series of questions in Gallup 1988 that would tap the attitudes toward and the practices employed in forgiving others. Answers to these questions will be used first to describe the role of forgiveness in the lives of Americans and to determine whether it makes any difference in people's lives. Finally, we will explore the relationship between prayer and the forgiveness process.

DOES IT PAY TO FORGIVE?

Some years ago a student-friend of one of the authors was murdered by an intruder who broke into the family home. The parents of this twenty-two-year-old college student proved to be remarkable in their ability to forgive. From the day they identified their son's body, this couple prayed daily for a forgiving spirit and for the opportunity to show their forgiveness to the one who had murdered their son. Their prayers were answered. Although they were not permitted to meet with the man who was alleged to have entered their home and killed their son until after his conviction, the long-awaited meeting did finally occur. The mother approached the man, took his hands into her own, and said quietly to him, "I do forgive you. Can you believe that I have come to love you like the son we lost?" The man broke down and wept.

While most Americans will never have to confront that level of hurt caused by another, all of us have experienced wounds from friends and family, acquaintances, and even strangers. The Gallup survey sought to learn more about people's attitudes and behavior when they have been wronged by another. Judging from the results, forgiveness is a well-accepted norm in our society.

The overwhelming majority of our respondents felt it was important for a religious person to forgive others who had deliberately injured him or her. When asked how important it was "for a religious person to make an effort to forgive others who have deliberately hurt them in some way," 94 percent agreed that it was fairly important or very important to offer such forgiveness. Just as the couple described earlier relied on prayer to be able to extend forgiveness to their son's murderer, the vast majority of Americans (83%) felt that God's help was needed to be able to truly forgive someone. Only a small minority felt they could forgive using only their own power and resources (15%).

Our data concur with the assertion of folk and religious wisdom that a forgiving spirit is a positive force. We tested for the effects that a positive attitude toward forgiveness may have on a person's life by looking at the relationship between attitudes toward forgiveness and the degree to which a person reported being satisfied with his or her life. As may be seen in Table 1, a positive attitude toward forgiveness is related to life satisfaction (r = .16). Those who felt it is important to forgive others who have deliberately hurt them are also more likely to be satisfied with their lives.

A belief that forgiveness is a good thing, however, does not mean that persons necessarily extend forgiveness to those who have wronged them. As may be seen from the percentages reported next to each item in Table 1, there are more people who *think* it is important to forgive than people who *actually try to forgive*. When asked what they usually do when someone has wronged them, only 48 percent of the respondents said they tried to forgive, slightly more than half of the 94 percent who felt it was fairly or very important for people to forgive others who have hurt them. Forgiveness appears to be more praised than practiced!

FORGIVING, SEEKING FORGIVENESS, AND LIFE SATISFACTION

In order to determine what it is that people do when they are deliberately injured, respondents were asked, "Which of these do you usually do when you feel that someone has done something wrong to you?" and were presented with eight possi-

TABLE 1
Relationship between Forgiveness Items and Satisfaction with Life

Which of the following do you usually do when you feel that someone has done something to wrong you?[+]

	N	Yes (%)	Correlation w/ Lifesat
Negative acts			
Try to get even	80	8	-.09[°]
Hold a resentment, or keep it inside	138	14	-.13[°]
NEGACT index			-.14[°]
Neutral act			
Try to overlook it, or push it out of one's mind	431	45	-.04
Positive acts			
Try to forgive the other person	465	48	.11[°]
Pray for that person	237	25	.19[°]
Pray to God for comfort and guidance	264	27	.03
Try to discuss the matter with the person to bring your feelings out into the open	462	48	.10[°]
Do something nice for the person	97	9	.04
POSACT index			.16[°]

How important do you think it is for a religious person to make an effort to forgive others who have deliberately hurt them in some way? .16[°]

	N	Yes (%)	
Not at all important	17	2	
Not too important	46	5	
Fairly important	278	29	
Very important	629	65	

TABLE 1 (*Continued*)

Positive acts	N	Yes (%)	Correlation w/ Lifesat
How strongly do you agree or disagree with this statement: to truly forgive someone from the heart for a serious hurt, one must rely on God's help?			.07
Strongly disagree	61	6	
Disagree	97	9	
Agree	341	36	
Strongly agree	449	47	

+ Respondents could select as many items as applied to them for these questions.

° Correlations for asterisk items are significant at $p = .001$ or less.

N = Number of respondents

Lifesat = Life Satisfaction Question: "On a scale of 1 to 7, with 1 being very dissatisfied, how satisfied are you with your life?"

ble courses of action. Since the items were not mutually exclusive, respondents were permitted to select as many answers as they felt described their likely response. Two of these responses were regarded as "negative," one as "neutral," and five as being "positive" in relation to forgiveness.[2] The negative acts (NEGACTs) included trying to get even and holding resentment. The positive acts (POSACTs) were trying to forgive, praying for the other person, asking God for comfort and guidance, trying to discuss the matter with the person, and doing something nice for the offender. The response which stood alone was one of mental repression—trying to overlook the wrong or push it out of mind.

2. These eight items were submitted to factor analysis and they loaded, as expected, on three separate factors. Cronbach's alpha for the two-item negative acts (NEGACTs) scale is .33; for the five-item positive acts (POSACTs) scale the reliability is .63. One item, a passive response considered to be "neutral," factored separately.

As may be seen in Table 1, relatively few persons claimed usually to try to get even (8%) or to deliberately harbor resentment (14%). What is significant, however, is that fewer of these respondents were likely to be satisfied with their lives than were those who did not try to get even or nurse resentments. The negative impact of a nonforgiving spirit is reflected in the correlations reported in the far right-hand column of Table 1. These correlations may be illustrated through the use of percentages not shown. Of those who sought revenge against wrong, only 19 percent claimed to be very satisfied with their lives, as compared with 25 percent who did not claim to try to get even.

The differences in life satisfaction are even greater between those 14 percent of the sample who chose to hold onto resentments and the vast majority who did not. The correlation of -.14 for the activities index may be described further using percentages not reported in Table 1. Fifteen percent of those who kept the resentment inside scored high on satisfaction with life in contrast to 25 percent of those who did not bury their resentment. Conversely 61 percent of the "resenters" scored low in life satisfaction, compared with 42 percent of those who took steps to let go of the hurt.

A near-majority of the respondents (45%) included in their repertoire the neutral item of trying to overlook the wrong by pushing it out of their minds. Unfortunately there is no way of knowing how respondents interpreted this question: it may have reflected a simple refusal to focus on the hurt (a potentially positive reaction) or it may have indicated burying or repressing it (a potentially negative response). This particular item had no effect on life satisfaction, although many used it in conjunction with other techniques for handling hurts.

Most respondents indicated multiple choices to describe their reactions to being hurt. For example, 44 percent of those who indicated that they tried to forgive the person who had wronged them also tried not to dwell on the hurt. Others who indicated that they tried to forgive the offender tended to combine this desire with other positive steps, the modal one being an attempt to bring feelings out into the open by discussing the matter. Over half of those who tried to forgive the offender (52%) also discussed the problem with the offender. Over a third of those who tried to forgive combined this determinism with prayer, either prayer for the offender (37%) or prayer for personal comfort (39%). The least chosen course of action was to "do something nice for the person," with only 16 percent of those who tried to forgive also being willing to go the extra mile to achieve reconciliation.

Given our earlier finding that those who felt it was important to be forgiving were also more likely to be satisfied with their lives, it was not surprising to find a positive correlation between acts of forgiveness and life satisfaction. As may be seen in the far right-hand column of Table 1, three of the five "positive acts" were directly related to life satisfaction scores. Although the "neutral" response of repression or not dwelling on the hurt was not correlated with life satisfaction, the two "negative acts" were negatively related to our dependent variable.

To sum up our findings to this point, those who believe in the importance of forgiveness appear to be more satisfied with their lives. This relationship between forgiveness and life satisfaction received additional support when considered with responses to the question asking what the respondent usually did "when you feel that someone has done something wrong to you." Those who tried to get even or held a resentment ("negative acts") were less likely to be satisfied than the overall sample. Similarly, those who tried to forgive, who prayed, and who discussed the matter with the offender were more likely to be satisfied than the overall sample. Simply trying to overlook the wrong by pushing it out of mind, which could have represented a healthy "letting go" or a less healthy act of repression, did not show a relationship with life satisfaction. Forgiveness is more than an empty proverb; it seems to work—at least to effect greater satisfaction with one's life.

Before leaving the topic of forgiveness and life satisfaction, we wanted to explore which of these eight responses were really responsible for changes in life satisfaction scores. This is especially critical given the fact that people could and did give multiple responses to the question dealing with handling being hurt. Multiple regression analysis, a statistical technique used in early chapters, was again employed as a control for interaction among choices. When all eight of the choices were entered as independent variables and satisfaction with life was the selected dependent variable, only two "choices" were statistically significant. Holding a resentment was negatively related and praying for the offender was positively related to life satisfaction scores.[3]

The finding fits well with an attitudinal response reported earlier. The vast majority of Americans felt that God's assistance was required to be able "to truly forgive someone from the heart" (see Table 1). Our data strongly suggest that forgiveness reaps positive benefits. Those who take positive measures to forgive wrongs are definitely more satisfied with their lives than those who do not. The positive step that is most effective involves a particular form of prayer. Those who are able to follow Jesus' teaching to "love your enemies and pray for those who persecute you" (Matt. 5:44) are those who reap the rewards of a more satisfied life.[4]

3. The R square for this equation was .06, with a significance of .0001. The individual betas for the two statistically significant items are as follows: "hold a resentment" = -.12; and "pray for the offender" = .17. All other nonsignificant betas were .04 or less.

4. As would be expected, praying for the offending party is somewhat correlated to other possible response choices. The Pearsonian correlations for "praying for the wrong-doer" and other response choices are as follows: "get even" = -.11; "hold resentment inside" = -.06; "overlook it" = -.02; "forgive" = .31; "pray for comfort" = .32; "discuss matter with offender" = .47; and "do something nice" = .09.

PRAYER, THE PRAY-ER,
AND FORGIVENESS

Most Americans appear at least to try to act in positive ways when injured by another.[5] Only 19 percent of the respondents identified one of the two negative acts as a way they normally responded to being hurt. On the other hand, approximately 75 percent of the respondents chose at least one positive or "healthy" act as a normal response. Only 3 percent engaged in all five positive acts, with the modal category being a combination of two positive choices (36%).

We would like to take a closer look at the respondents who were most likely to go the extra mile in forgiving—those who prayed, who sought reconciliation through discussion, and who rewarded those who injured them with a kind act.

Table 2 presents the bivariate relationships between forgiveness and select demographic and religious variables. The demographics of age, sex, race, and education demonstrate weak bivariate relationships with positive responses to injury; age, sex, and education (but not race) are negatively correlated with negative responses. It appears that older persons, women, whites, and those with less education are a bit more likely to engage in positive responses to being hurt than are younger persons, men, non-whites, and those with more education. Similarly, younger persons, men, and those with less education are more likely to engage in negative responses to being hurt than are older persons, women, and those with more education. Although statistically significant, these relationships are judged

5. They also perceive themselves as trying to right their own wrongs against others. Respondents were asked what they usually did when they had "done wrong to someone." An overwhelming majority claimed to apologize (80%), and a near majority (46%) claimed to "try to improve relations with that person by doing something kind." Apologizing does not seem to necessarily include "asking the other person's forgiveness"; only 42 percent claimed that as a usual response. A little over one-third of the respondents (35%) asked for God's forgiveness. Of particular interest is that *only the prayerful act of seeking God's forgiveness was related to life satisfaction scores (r = .10)*; the other responses were not statistically significant.

TABLE 2
Zero-Order Correlations for Forgiveness Items and Select Variables

	BEHAVIOR			ATTITUDES	
	Positive Action	Negative Action	Neutral Response (No Action)	Importance of Forgiveness	Need God to Forgive
Age	.10	-.16	-.08	.11	.16
Sex°	.14	-.08	ns	.12	.11
Race+	-.08	ns	-.07	ns	ns
Education	-.08	-.07	.10	-.09	-.17
Income	ns	ns	ns	ns	ns
Importance of Religion	.39	-.18	-.09	.37	.51
Member	.26	-.11	ns	.24	.32
Attend	.27	-.08	-.08	.20	.24
Evangelical	.38	-.08	-.10	.28	.37
Charismatic	.28	-.08	-.10	.17	.20
Relation to God	.39	-.20	-.15	.37	.44
Pray	.20	ns	ns	.24	.45
Petitionary	.19	ns	-.09	.10	.20
Meditative	.36	-.14	ns	.31	.37
Colloquial	.29	-.09	ns	.22	.34
Ritual	ns	-.08	ns	ns	ns
Prayer Experience	.41	-.13	-.11	.26	.40
Lifesat	.16	-.14	ns	.16	.08
POSACT	—	-.10	ns	.28	.34
NEGACT	-.09	—	ns	-.13	-.08
Neutral	ns	ns	—	-.10	ns
Importance of Forgiveness	.32	-.14	-.10	—	.41
God's Help	.37	-.09	-.12	.41	—

° A positive score indicates a higher score for female than male respondents.

+ A negative score indicates a higher score for white than black respondents.

NOTE: All zero-order correlations are significant at $p = .01$ or higher.

ns = not significant.

to be weak.[6] Much stronger predictors of a forgiving spirit may be found in the religious variables used in this survey.

With the exception of one prayer type (ritual prayer), all of the religiosity measures are positively correlated with positive responses to injury. Especially strong correlations are found between acts of forgiveness and scores on the prayer experience scale ($r = .41$), religious salience ($r = .39$), feeling very close to God ($r = .39$), being born-again ($r = .38$), and meditative prayer ($r = .36$). A more descriptive table showing the relationship between religiosity and forgiveness may be seen in the percentages presented in Table 3.

Of those who reported religion was "very important" to them, only 16 percent scored low in positive responses to injury as compared with 52 percent who scored high.[7] Forty-six percent of church members scored high on positive responses as compared with 25 percent of nonmembers. Sixty-two percent of the respondents who scored high on prayer experiences (versus 25 percent who scored low) also scored high on positive responses to injury.

A similar pattern (although with weaker correlations) may be observed in the second and third columns under "Behavior" in Table 2, which relate negative forms of action and neutral responses with religiosity measures. Those who find religion less important, who feel more distant from God, and who have

6. The five demographic variables were able to explain only 3 percent of the variance in POSACT scores. The two variables that were statistically significant in this multiple regression equation were sex and race. Women were somewhat more likely than men to be forgiving (beta = .17), and whites more likely than non-whites (beta = .15).

The demographic variables explained 4 percent of the variance in negative responses to being injured. Age (beta = -.15) and being male (beta = .12) were positively related to NEGACT. The three other demographic variables were not statistically significant.

7. Low scores were given to the 25 percent of the respondents who did not engage in any "positive acts" as a normal response to deliberate injury. The 36 percent who reported one "positive act" was categorized as medium. Those who indicated two to five items that reflected a forgiving spirit were categorized as high on the scale.

TABLE 3
Healthy Responses to Injury by Select
Religiosity Measures

RELIGIOSITY MEASURES	FORGIVENESS INDEX		
	Low	Medium	High
Importance of Religion			
Very	16%	33%	52%
Fairly	30%	41%	29%
Not Very	48%	42%	10%
Church Membership			
Yes	19%	35%	46%
No	37%	39%	25%
Born-again			
Yes	12%	29%	59%
No	30%	39%	32%
Meditative Prayer			
Yes	14%	33%	53%
No	30%	38%	33%
Prayer Experience Index			
Low	32%	43%	25%
Medium	18%	36%	47%
High	10%	28%	62%

---

fewer prayer experiences are more likely to seek revenge or to hold resentments than those who are more religious. Religiosity was also negatively related to choosing the neutral act as a response to being injured. Those who tried to overlook the matter—to put it out of mind through either repression or an unwillingness to dwell on the hurt—were less likely to be very religious.

Of particular interest to us is the relationship between prayer and forgiveness. Whether or not a person prays shows a moderate bivariate correlation (r = .20) with a positive response to injury but is not statistically related to negative or neutral responses. As may be seen from Table 2, however, three of the four prayer activities (meditative, colloquial, and ritual) show negative bivariate relationships with NEGACT. In other words, those who engage in these forms of prayer are more likely to respond in a healthy manner when wronged than those who do not so engage themselves. It appears that whether or not persons pray is less important than the kind of prayer in which they engage.

The bivariate correlations between type of prayer and POSACT are clarified by using multiple regression techniques to distinguish the effects of the different prayer forms. Meditative pray-ers are significantly more likely to demonstrate forgiveness when wronged and less likely to nurture resentments than are those who rely solely on more active forms of prayer.[8] When the effects of the prayer-items on positive responses to injury were analyzed using multiple regression techniques (which put the needed statistical controls into place), prayer

8. R square for the equation in which POSACT was regressed on the four types of prayer is .10. Statistically significant betas were found for colloquial (beta = .15) and meditative (beta = .24) prayer forms.

Only 3 percent of the variance for NEGACT was explained by the different forms of prayer. Colloquial (beta = .10) and meditative (beta = .10) were both negatively related to unhealthy responses to being deliberately hurt by another.

experience was found to be a leading "cause" of forgiveness. There were some other variables, however, that also contribute to the description of a "forgiving person." The portrait of such a person would show a white woman who says religion is very important to her, who engages in meditative prayer, and who has frequent encounters with God during prayer.[9] While these statistics may be convincing to some, they lack a human dimension. A case study may help to illustrate the process behind the numbers.

DIVINE INTIMACY AND FORGIVENESS:
A CASE STUDY

Far more Americans regard forgiveness as a virtue than are able or willing to forgive. Judging from our data, we would anticipate that the ability to forgive is positively related to prayer, particularly to meditative prayer and to the experiences of God during prayer. Many readers may wonder why the spirit of forgiveness is so strong in Americans but the flesh of positive responses to injury so weak. Perhaps an incident recounted to one of the authors may help provide a greater understanding of what the numbers appear to be saying.

Chris, a single parent in her mid-thirties, was trying to finish her college degree to provide a better life for herself and her two children. Her husband was a violent man who repeatedly abused her and the children, and his violence forced her to abandon their affluent lifestyle in Florida to make her way back to the Midwest and onto public assistance. Despite the fact that her husband was a millionaire, he refused to pay the alimony and child support ordered by the courts. Her bitterness and

9. The R square for POSACT when the four prayer types and religious experience are entered as independent variables is .13. When the demographics, religious salience, and ritual measures are added to the prayer items, the explained variance increases to R square = .17. Significant betas were found for being female (.13), being white (.17), religious salience (.12), meditative prayer (.13), and prayer experiences (.16).

deep hatred of him were understandable but also seemed to be contributing to deep personal bouts of depression.

One morning during prayer she felt the Lord was leading her to read and pray with the parable of the unforgiving servant (Matt. 18:21-35). In this account, Jesus told the story of a master who threatened a servant who owed him a good sum of money with being tossed into debtor's prison. The servant begged for mercy and the master forgave the debt. This same servant had a fellow servant who owed him a much smaller amount. The co-worker to no avail asked his creditor to be patient, but instead he was thrown into prison. When the master found out what had happened, he was angry with the unforgiving servant and "turned him over to the jailers until he should pay back all he owed." Jesus then said, "This is how my heavenly Father will treat each of you unless you forgive your brother from your heart."

Chris was deeply moved by this parable during this time of prayer. As an evangelical Christian very familiar with the Bible, she knew the story well—but it had never touched her as it did this day. She felt Jesus was telling her that her depression was the prison into which she had thrust herself as a result of her unwillingness to forgive her ex-husband. She began to weep and to ask for the grace to be able to forgive him. That prayer encounter was a turning point in Chris's life—one during which the process of forgiveness and healing began. She was able to let go of the resentments toward her husband and gradually to go on with her life without the pain of chronic depression.

Religion was very important to Chris, and she attended church regularly, read the Bible, and had a time set aside for daily prayer. Her prayer was far from being rote or being a one-sided monologue. She tried to listen for what she believed to be the voice of God and then to obey the instructions. Turning to the parable of the unforgiving servant was the catalyst of a religious experience that precipitated a desire to forgive her ex-husband. This willingness to forgive rather than to continue to nurture the past hurts seemed to bring Chris to a greater psychological wholeness. Chris's story suggests a model which allows us to summarize our findings.

RELIGIOSITY AND FORGIVENESS: A MODEL AND SUMMARY

We have suggested and attempted to test two basic ideas in this chapter: (1) forgiving those who have deliberately done wrong has a positive effect on well-being, and (2) prayer is the single most important factor in explaining why some persons are better able than others to forgive those who have wronged them. It is the second point that is especially relevant to the topic of this book and one that we would like to illustrate through the model provided in Figure 1.

As may be seen from a close examination of the correlations provided in Table 2, almost all of the religiosity measures are related to forgiveness. At the same time these measures are related to each other. Can any order be given to all these measures that would help us to better understand the process of forgiveness? Figure 1 presents such a model to depict the causal relationships between forgiveness and different religious expressions and acts.[10]

The model begins with the answer to the question, "How important is religion to you?" It assumes that religious salience will "cause" a person (just as it caused Chris) to engage in certain religious acts, specifically public ritual (church attendance) and private devotion (prayer). The bivariate correlation for ritual and religious salience ($r = .46$) demonstrates that indeed those for whom religion is very important are more likely to

10. Those unfamiliar with modeling and statistics may disregard the numbers found in Fig. 1 except to note that they designate the statistically significant relationships. The numbers show statistically significant betas between items linked by the arrows; "ns" indicates that the path was "not significant."

FIGURE 1
A Causal Model for Religiosity and Forgiveness

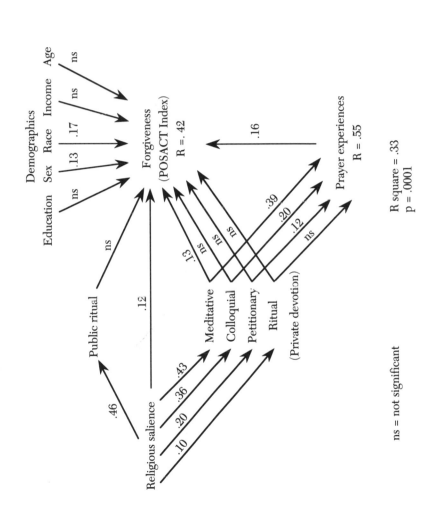

attend church. They are also more likely to engage in all four of the different prayer activities, with the strongest correlation existing between meditative prayer and religious salience ($r = .43$). Only those who pray will have prayer experiences, but the forms of praying may have direct or indirect effects (through prayer experiences) on positive responses to injury (POSACT).

Through the use of multiple regression we were able to sort out the "interaction effects" (i.e., those effects which appear to be caused by one variable but which are actually due to another). We saw in Table 2, for example, that most demographics and most religiosity measures (including the different prayer items) affect healthy responses to being wronged. Some of them undoubtedly interact with one another (e.g., older persons are more likely to be female), making it difficult to determine the real "cause." Furthermore, religious salience, ritual, and devotion may interact with each other and with the demographic variables. Multiple regression techniques are able to take these concerns into account in order to determine whether prayer (and/or some other variables) actually accounts for the differences we found in POSACT scores.

The model presented in Figure 1 indicates that religious salience (beta = .12), being female (beta = .13), and being white (beta = .17) all have some effects on positive acts of forgiveness. With other variables acting as controls, church attendance was found to have no relationship to POSACT. Private devotion, measured by the four types of prayer, has an indirect effect on POSACT—those who pray are the only ones who can have prayer experiences, and some forms of prayer are more likely to lead to such experiences than others. Meditation, a more passive form of prayer, has both direct and indirect effects on positive responses to injury. It is the only prayer form that links directly to POSACT (beta = .13) and demonstrates the strongest direct relationship (beta = .39) with prayer experiences. Encountering God during prayer or prayer experience is the leading "cause" of an ability to forgive (beta = .16). It appears that meditative pray-ers, whether or not they have frequent and varied prayer experiences, are the most likely people to respond positively to deliberate injury.

Our discussion of forgiveness in this chapter is consistent with the findings reported in earlier chapters. Prayer is an important part of the lives of Americans, and it appears to have positive effects in their lives. In the next chapter we will continue to explore some functions of prayer by considering its relationship to what it means to be religious.

WORKS CITED

Bonar, Clyde A.
    1989   Personality Theories and Asking Forgiveness. *Journal of Psychology and Christianity* 8:45–51.

Brink, T.L.
    1985   The Role of Religion in Later Life: A Case of Consolation and Forgiveness. *Journal of Psychology and Christianity* 4:22–25.

Darby, Bruce, and Barry R. Schlenker
    1982   Children's Reactions to Apologies. *Journal of Personality and Social Psychology* 43:742–53.

Enright, Robert D., Maria J. Santos, and Radhi Al-Mabuk
    1989   The Adolescent as Forgiver. *Journal of Adolescence* 12:95–110.

Fitzgibbons, Richard P.
    1986   The Cognitive and Emotive Uses of Forgiveness in the Treatment of Anger. *Psychotherapy* 23 (4):629–35.

Hope, Donald L.
    1987   The Healing Paradox of Forgiveness. *Psychotherapy* 24(2):240–44.

Kaufman, Morton E.
    1984   The Courage to Forgive. *Journal of Psychiatry and Relational Sciences* 21:177–87.

Parsons, Richard D.
    1988   Forgiving-not-Forgetting. *Psychotherapy Patient* 5:259–73.

Pattison, E. Mansell
  1965   On the Failure to Forgive or Be Forgiven. *American Journal of Psychotherapy* 19:106–15.
Pingleton, Jared P.
  1989   The Role and Function of Forgiveness in the Psychotherapeutic Process. *Journal of Psychology and Theology* 17:27–35.
Ritzman, Thomas A.
  1987   Forgiveness: Its Role in Therapy. *Medical Hypnoanalysis Journal* 2:4–13.
Roloff, Michael E., and Chris A. Janiszewski
  1989   Overcoming Obstacles to Interpersonal Compliance: A Principle of Message Construction. *Human Communication Research* 16:33–61.
Rosenzweig-Smith, Janet
  1988   *Factors Associated with Successful Reunions of Adult Adoptees and Biological Parents.* Trenton: New Jersey Department of Human Services, Office of Analysis, Evaluation, and Strategic Planning.
Shontz, Franklin C., and Charlotte Rosenak
  1988   Psychological Theories and the Need for Forgiveness: Assessment and Critique. *Journal of Psychology and Christianity* 7:23–31.

6

TO COMFORT OR
TO CHALLENGE
Prayer and Approaches to Religion

A wise man will always be a Christian, because the perfection of wisdom is to know where lies tranquility of mind, and how to attain it, which Christianity teaches.

— Walter Savage Landor

No man [is a Christian] . . . who does not think constantly of how he can lift his brother, how he can assist his friend, how he can enlighten mankind, how he can make virtue the rule of conduct in the circle in which he lives.

— Woodrow Wilson

In observing the religious revival that appears to be underway as we close the twentieth century, some social scientists have responded critically, insisting that the many faces of renewed interest in religion are simply reflections of the narcissism inherent in our culture. These social critics insist that many turn to religion for comfort but ignore the challenge found in the Judeo-Christian scriptures. Religious believers are often assumed to use their faith to seek "tranquility of mind" but are less prone to use it to "lift [their] brother."

The topic of "to comfort" or "to challenge" has received

considerable attention in social science literature. Of particular note is the vast amount of research on "intrinsic" and "extrinsic" religiosity that built upon the famed social psychologist Gordon Allport's (1950) attempts to identify and contrast the traits of mature and immature religion. No psychological approach to the empirical study of religion has received more attention than Allport's famous typology (Donahue, 1985).

Intrinsic religiosity is characterized by a devout, strong personal commitment, while extrinsic religiosity is rule-oriented and called on largely in times of crisis. While extrinsic religiosity is allegedly exclusionist, ethnocentric, and provincial, intrinsic religiosity is universalistic, stressing the need to love all persons. In other words, intrinsically religious people are unselfish, altruistic, and humanitarian. Extrinsically religious people are selfish, self-serving, defensive, and protective. For intrinsically religious people, faith is of ultimate significance, providing a guide to living. For the extrinsically religious, faith is superficial and is "used when needed" rather than integrated into their daily lives (Spilka et al., 1985:19). While extrinsic religion may comfort followers, it is an intrinsic approach to religion that supposedly provides the challenge.

Research done on the intrinsic-extrinsic framework led a collaborator on this Gallup survey, psychologist Richard L. Gorsuch, to include on it three items representing different approaches to religion. Two extrinsic questions were included, the first to measure the social dimension and the second to tap a personal dimension: (1) "I go to church mainly to spend time with my friends," and (2) "What religion offers me most is comfort in times of trouble and sorrow." The measure of intrinsic motivation Gorsuch calls "age-universal" was tapped by the following statement: "My whole approach to life is based on my religion" (Kennedy and Gorsuch, 1989). Gorsuch's measures of the intrinsic-extrinsic typology are indicators of motivation, seeking to determine whether religious acts are spurred by social rewards (friendships) or personal rewards (comfort), or whether religion is a universal force (motivator) that permeates the believer's life.

The intrinsic-extrinsic typology as found in the social science literature reflects more than religious motivation. A multifaceted (and often imprecisely defined) concept, it has been used to designate religious *motivation, orientation, commitment, cognitive style,* and *personality type* (Kirkpatrick and Hood, 1989). In other words, indicators commonly tap only one facet of what it means to be religious. The questions used by Gorsuch, for example, seem to deal with different types of religious motivation. Other measures may reflect other facets of so-called intrinsic and extrinsic religiosity.

Another approach to identifying different interpretations of what it means to be religious is to ask respondents their opinions of what makes a "good Christian or Jew," an approach that reflects religious orientation. Four questions were used to identify what we call "institutional" and "conscience-based" forms of religious orientation. Respondents were asked to indicate on a five-point scale the strength of their agreement or disagreement with each of the following characteristics of a "good Christian or Jew":

1. to attend regularly religious services at a church or synagogue
2. to believe in God without question or doubt
3. to follow faithfully the teachings of a church or synagogue
4. to follow your conscience even if it means going against what the churches and synagogues say and do.

A factor analysis of these four items showed the first three clustering together, permitting us to use them as a single index reflecting institutional orientation. The fourth item stood alone as a measure of conscience orientation.[1]

As may be seen in Table 1, respondents varied in their self-attributed religious motivation and in their views on religious orientation. A clear majority (64%) strongly disagreed with the statement "I go to church or synagogue mainly to spend time with my friends." On the other hand, a near majority (42%) strongly agreed with the statement "What religion offers me most is comfort in times of trouble and sorrow." Responses were slightly skewed toward agreement with the item measuring an intrinsic approach to religion: "My whole approach to life is based on my religion." Responses were nearly evenly dispersed for the index measuring institutional commitment, with 19 percent indicating strong support for an institutional approach to religion and 21 percent taking a strong stand against our institutional criteria of belief, regular church attendance, and following the teaching of the churches. The responses to the item measuring a highly individualistic approach which we termed "conscience orientation" were skewed negatively. Thirty-four percent strongly disagreed that being a religious person is characterized by "following your conscience even if it means going against what the churches and synagogues say and do." Although such privatization of religion is sometimes described as being prevalent in American society (cf. Bellah et al., 1985), only a minority of respondents (17%) strongly agreed that exclusive reliance on one's personal conscience is a mark of a "good Christian or Jew."

What the data presented in Table 1 suggest is that religiosity means different things to different people. For a minority, the social predominates; for others, institutional concerns are paramount; for still others, it is a privatized and personal con-

---

1. A Cronbach's alpha to determine reliability was also run on the items. The reliability for the three institutional items is alpha = .82.

TABLE 1
Frequencies for Religious Motivation
and Orientation

	Strongly Disagree				Strongly Agree
Religious Motivation	1	2	3	4	5
Religion offers comfort (extrinsic personal)	8%	7%	20%	23%	42%
Attend church for friends (extrinsic social)	64%	16%	10%	5%	6%
Whole life religion based (age universal)	18%	12%	25%	19%	26%
Religious Orientation					
Institutional Index	19%	21%	20%	18%	21%
Attend church	29%	15%	19%	15%	23%
Believe without doubt	44%	11%	11%	11%	22%
Follow church's teachings	27%	18%	19%	17%	20%
Conscience-based	34%	17%	20%	13%	17%

science. The question we raise is whether any of these forms of religiosity are "better" than others. Are some approaches to religion more "mature" (i.e., do they "bear more fruit") than others?

To explore this question, we considered the effects of intrinsic and extrinsic religious motivation and institutional and conscience orientation on some of the issues analyzed in earlier chapters. Of particular interest was the relationship between the different types of religiosity and (1) political activism, (2) forgiveness, and (3) life satisfaction. We then took a closer look at the role played by prayer types and prayer experiences in shaping religious motivation and commitment. In the section that follows we attempt to identify what appears to be the more mature approaches to faith.

TO COMFORT *AND* TO CHALLENGE: ORIENTATION AND MOTIVATION

Our measures of religious motivation and orientation have some surprising effects on our dependent variables of life satisfaction, forgiveness, and political activism. Table 2 provides a summary of the findings in the form of bivariate correlations in the lower section of the table with some select descriptive percentages at the upper portion of the table. These findings deserve further discussion.

What Makes a "Good Christian or Jew"?

Our two measures of religious orientation reflect what people consider to be the attributes of a "good Christian or Jew": some favor the institutional emphasis on doctrine and ritual, while others side with a conscience-based orientation. Opinions on these two religious orientations seem to have no positive effects on the dependent variables; in fact, they often are negatively related to our dependent measures. Thus, personal religiosity that is based on individual conscience rather than on religious authority has no significant relationship with life satisfaction, forgiveness, or political activism. Institutional religiosity demonstrates statistically significant relationships with forgiveness and local political activism, but these are negative relationships. In other words, people who had higher scores on the institutional index (e.g., a good Christian or Jew believes in God with certainty, attends church or synagogue, and follows religious teachings) scored no differently on life satisfaction than those who were less institutional in orientation. They were, however, less likely to become involved in politics, and they were less likely to respond positively when deliberately

TABLE 2
Religious Motivation/Orientation by
Forgiveness/Life Satisfaction

	Life Satisfaction			Forgiveness		
	Low	Medium	High	Low	Medium	High
Motivation						
Extrinsic social (friends)						
Disagree	44%	29%	28%	21%	35%	44%
Agree	44%	35%	21%	25%	41%	34%
Extrinsic personal (comfort)						
Disagree	50%	30%	19%	30%	39%	31%
Agree	38%	29%	32%	14%	34%	51%
Intrinsic-Universal (all life)						
Disagree	49%	29%	22%	32%	45%	23%
Agree	34%	33%	33%	16%	31%	54%
Orientation						
Institutional						
Disagree	40%	29%	31%	16%	32%	52%
Agree	43%	32%	26%	26%	41%	33%
Conscience-based						
Disagree	43%	31%	26%	20%	36%	44%
Agree	38%	33%	30%	28%	35%	37%

PEARSONIAN CORRELATIONS[*]

	Institutional	Conscientious	Friends	Comfort	Life
Life Satisfaction	ns	ns	ns	.12	.15
NEGACT (forgive)	.07	ns	ns	-.07	-.14
POSACT (forgive)	-.13	ns	-.12	.16	.30
Candidate (politics)	-.10	ns	ns	.12	.25
National Problems (politics)	ns	ns	ns	.09	.10

[*]All reported correlation coefficients are significant at the .01 level or less.

ns = not significant

injured by another person. For example, we see from Table 2 that while 52 percent of those who disagreed with the institutional orientation scale scored "high" on positive acts of forgiveness, only 33 percent of those whose image of a good Christian or Jew was institutionally oriented scored high on forgiveness.

What are we to make of this? It appears that the general orientation toward religion has little or no positive impact on respondents' lives. Our data indicate that these two major orientations—institutional and highly personal—have only very weak relationships with the religiosity measures of church attendance, religious salience, and prayer.[2] In other words, the orientation that a person has toward being a "good" Christian or "good" Jew may reflect perceptions of cultural norms and values, but it appears to have only tenuous relationships to traditional measures of religiosity. Furthermore, although a privatized conscience orientation to religion may sound good to some, it does not reap the fruits expected of a mature religious faith. A rigid institutional approach to religion fares even worse. Those who claim to favor the importance of institutional traits over personal ones in classifying a "good Christian or Jew" are less likely to engage in positive acts and more likely to revert to negative ones when deliberately injured by another.

Religious Motivators:
Intrinsic or Extrinsic

The items included by Richard Gorsuch in this survey were designed to reflect personal intrinsic, social intrinsic, and

2. The correlations for conscientious orientation and select religious measures are as follows: church attendance, .06; religious salience, -.10; meditative prayer, .06; prayer experiences, .01; and perceived closeness to God, .09. For institutional orientation the correlations are: church attendance, .17; religious salience, .23; meditative prayer, .07; prayer experiences, -.12; and closeness to God, -.17.

One interesting finding in these correlations: those who ignore church authority in favor of their consciences indicate that religion is less important to them than it is to those who are institutionally oriented. Paradoxically, however, those who score high on institutional orientations, despite their emphasis on the importance of religion in their lives, are less likely to feel a closeness to God or to experience God in prayer than are those who score somewhat lower.

extrinsic (universal) religious motivation. The correlations on the lower half of Table 2 reflect some basic differences among these motivators. What is apparent from even a cursory glance is that social motivatation to attend church has no impact on life satisfaction or religiously motivated political involvement. We were surprised to find that those who were socially motivated to attend church (i.e., went primarily for friendship) were less likely to respond to injury in positive ways. The inability of "extrinsic social" types (to use Gorsuch's term) to respond in healthy ways to being hurt fits well with earlier findings suggesting that extrinsic religiosity is a less "mature" form of religion than is intrinsic.

But we can also see from these correlations that Gorsuch is correct when he insists on the distinction between what he calls "personal" and "social" forms of extrinsic religiosity. Those who find religion to be a great comfort to them are more likely to be satisfied with their lives, less likely to respond negatively and more likely to respond positively when injured by another, and more likely to be involved in both national and local politics out of a religious concern. As we can see from Table 2, for example, 32 percent of those who strongly agreed that religion was a source of comfort to them scored high on life satisfaction as compared with 19 percent of those who did not find religion personally comforting. Similarly, 51 percent of those who found religion a great comfort scored high on positive acts of forgiveness in contrast to 31 percent who did not find comfort in religion.

What our data suggest is that religion may be both comforting and challenging. The positive effects of its comforting power may be seen in the increase in life satisfaction scores. But the comfort received from religion may also provide challenges as reflected in the increased scores in both political activism and the ability to forgive when deliberately wronged.

This same pattern, but with somewhat stronger correlations, is found for the "intrinsic" or "age universal" religiosity measure which asks if the respondent's "whole approach to life is based on religion." As may be seen from the correlations presented in Table 2, those for whom religion is a universal motivator are even more likely to be satisfied with their lives, respond positively when deliberately injured, and be politically active.

What we have attempted to do with the information available from our survey is to identify which approach to religion is the most "mature" in terms of the effects it has on respondents' lives. It appears that an intrinsic religious motivation that permeates the believer's entire life is the approach that bears the most fruit. It also appears that this path offers comfort together with challenge. There is a blending of a privatized comforting faith with the challenge of faith in action. Those whose approach to religion is mainly social, heavily institutional, or dictated solely by conscience appear to reap little of the comfort or the challenge offered to other believers.

What we would like to do in the next section is to explore the relationship between prayer and the approaches to religion we have identified. Does prayer have a role in the development of a more "mature" religious orientation? If it does, what form of prayer is the most likely to be related to spiritual maturity?

PRAYER AND APPROACHES TO FAITH

Less Mature Approaches
to Religiosity

Based on the analysis just presented, we would suggest that institutional and conscience orientations as well as extrinsic socially motivated approaches to religion all represent "less mature" forms of faith. In terms of the evidence collected in this survey, an extreme institutional loyalty, a regard for conscience apart from religious authority, and a socially dictated religious motivation all fail to contribute to the respondent's quality of life, to a mature moral stance, or to religiously motivated political activities. We were interested in learning whether prayer is in any way related to these religious types.

The first three columns of Table 3 report the bivariate relations for our prayer measures and these "less mature" approaches to religion. These bivariate relations suggest that

TABLE 3
Bivariate Correlations for
Religious Orientation and Motivation

	Orientation		Motivation		
	Institutional	Conscience	Social	Comfort	Life
Types of Prayer					
Petitionary	ns	ns	.09	.10	.18
Ritual	ns	ns	ns	ns	.09
Colloquial	ns	ns	ns	.18	.25
Meditative	-.12+	ns	ns	.26+	.37+
Prayer Experiences	-.12+	ns	ns	.18	.40+
Demographic Variables					
Education	ns	-.11°	-.08	-.13°	-.09
Sex	ns	ns	-.07°	.15	.15
Race	ns	.10	.12°	.08	.08
Income	ns	ns	ns	ns	ns
Age	-.08°	ns	.08°	.16°	.18°

All reported correlation coefficients are significant at the .01 level or less.

+ When the prayer measures are used as independent variables in multiple regression coefficients, with demographic variables held constant, the betas for the relationships noted with a + remain statistically significant.

° When each of the religious types was regressed against the demographic variables in multiple regression analysis, the betas for the ° items retained their statistical significance.

ns = not significant

prayer is largely unrelated to socially motivated and con-science-oriented religious types. There is, however, a negative bivariate relationship between meditative prayer and an institu-tional approach to religion.

The institutional posture that evaluates true religion by religious practices and beliefs is negatively related to two important prayer indicators. Those who strongly agree with an institutional approach to religion appear less likely to be people who pray meditatively. Perhaps more importantly, they are less likely to experience God in prayer than are those who are less institutionally oriented. For example, 69 percent of those who are low on institutionalism regularly employ meditative prayer practices as compared with 48 percent who score medium or high. Similarly, 44 percent of those who are less institutional in their approach to religion report having frequent prayer experi-ences in contrast to 34 percent who are high on institutional-ism.[3]

While not wishing to make too much out of this simple analysis, we do feel it demonstrates an important finding. While it appears that prayer does *not* account for two of these three "less mature" approaches to faith ("conscience" and "social" orientations), the negative relationship between mental prayer and an institutional approach to religion is worth noting. The findings are clearer and more interesting when we turn to the relationship between prayer and the "more mature" approaches to faith.

Prayer and Religious Maturity

In Table 2 we reported that those who found comfort in their faith as well as those for whom religion was central to their lives were more likely to report higher scores in life satisfaction, were more forgiving, and were more politically involved. Not

3. As noted in the + sign in Table 3, the negative relationship between prayer experi-ences and institutional approaches to religion holds up in multiple regression analysis in which the demographic measures are used as controls.

surprisingly, these respondents were also more likely to be men and women of prayer.

Most of the prayer items demonstrate statistically significant bivariate relationships with our two "more mature" faith forms (see the last two columns of Table 3.) Table 4 uses cross-tabular analysis to elaborate on the bivariate correlations reported earlier. For example, while only 29 percent of those who scored low on meditative prayer were likely to find religion a great source of comfort, 71 percent of those who scored high on meditative prayer were greatly comforted by their faith. The differences among the categories are most striking for the meditative prayer form, reflecting the stronger correlations reported in Table 3 for meditative prayer and for the two "mature" forms of religiosity.

We continued to pursue our analysis of the importance of prayer for more "mature" forms of religiosity by using multiple regression techniques. What we found is that prayer contributes much more toward "explaining" higher scores in intrinsic religiosity (universal motivation) than it does toward "explaining" extrinsic personal (comforting) motivation. Prayer measures were almost twice as important in helping to predict intrinsic religiosity as they were in predicting the extrinsic personal approach.[4] This analysis demonstrated further that meditative prayer was the prayer type responsible for explaining the differences we found. People who pray meditatively are likely to employ the other three prayer forms, a fact that accounts for the bivariate relationships reported in Table 3. But unless those other forms of prayer are supplemented with meditative prayer practices, they are unable to statistically account for differences in religious maturity.

4. The demographic items explain 4 percent of the variance for both approaches to religion. When the four prayer types were added to the multiple regression equation, the R square for extrinsic personal (comfort) was .09. The R square for the equation in which the intrinsic (universal importance) item was regressed against prayer and demographics was .18.

TABLE 4
Relationships between Mature Religiosity and Prayer Measures

	Extrinsic Personal (Comfort)			Intrinsic (Life)		
	Low	Medium	High	Low	Medium	High
Meditative Prayer						
Low	62%	49%	29%	71%	48%	27%
High	38%	51%	71%	29%	52%	73%
Colloquial Prayer						
Low	23%	19%	9%	30%	15%	9%
High	77%	81%	91%	70%	85%	91%
Ritual Prayer						
Low	84%	84%	77%	87%	80%	78%
High	16%	16%	23%	13%	20%	22%
Petitionary Prayer						
Low	64%	61%	52%	68%	62%	49%
High	36%	39%	49%	32%	39%	51%
Prayer Experiences						
Low	46%	27%	27%	57%	40%	18%
Medium	42%	35%	24%	26%	39%	30%
High	22%	32%	46%	17%	21%	52%

Our analysis of data in this chapter contained two steps: (1) an attempt to identify "mature" and "immature" forms of religion, and (2) an attempt to explore the relationship of these forms of religion to prayer. Although we realize our measures have not exhausted the different types of religiosity, they do demonstrate that different approaches to faith have differing results. Some forms of religion are more likely to bear fruit than are others. These more "mature" forms are fed by prayer, particularly meditative prayer, which is more likely to allow for intimate experiences with God. While the overwhelming majority of Americans claim to pray, not all approaches to prayer have the same effects. The more passive form of meditative prayer demonstrates a clear relationship to more "mature" approaches to faith.

NOT EVERYONE WHO SAYS "LORD, LORD!"

A strong personal religious faith is an important part of the identity of most Americans. For example, over half (53%) say that religion is *very* important to them, and over half say that religion can answer all or most of today's problems (Gallup and Jones, 1989:208, 212). Gallup surveys indicate that the majority (56%) say that "growing into a deeper relationship with God" is *very* important to them, with only a minority (16%) saying that it is not important. Although many people seem to be hungering for a deeper spirituality, they are not necessarily seeking strong ties with an institutional religiosity. This spiritual but not necessarily institutional approach is revealed by responses to a Gallup question which asked: "Which of the following four statements comes closest to your own view of 'faith': a set of beliefs, membership in a church or synagogue, finding meaning in life, or a relationship with God?" The majority (51%) chose a "relationship with God." Intermediate choices were "finding meaning in life" (20%) and "a set of beliefs" (19%), with church membership clearly being the least favored choice (4%) (Gallup and Jones, 1989:186–87).

This relationship with God desired by so many is reportedly nurtured by prayer. When asked, "What sort of things, if any, do you do to nourish or strengthen your faith?" 59 percent chose "pray alone" (*Emerging Trends*, 1983:1). Further evidence that prayer plays a major role in the lives of many Americans is seen by survey results that show 60 percent saying prayer is "very important" to them, while another 22 percent say it is "fairly important." Only 15 percent claim that prayer is "not very" or "not at all important" in their lives (*Emerging Trends*, 1985:1).

The analysis we presented in this chapter fits well with all of these earlier findings, suggesting further that such spiritual hunger is a reflection of a mature religious faith that often bears fruit. Wishing alone, however, does not satisfy the desire for God. Prayer, particularly meditative prayer, appears to play an important role in providing the "connection" between God and the praying person.

It is the more passive approach to prayer—a "being still and knowing he is God"—that seems to facilitate prayer experiences which in turn are the best indicators of healthy spirituality and religiously motivated activities. Prayer, especially in its meditative form, makes a difference! This more passive form of prayer sets the stage for religious experience—a time of intimacy with the Divine which seems to be a requisite for mature forms of faith.

As we have demonstrated in this chapter, a mature religious faith necessarily goes beyond formal religion. At the same time, it is not completely distinct from institutional religious expressions. Human beings as social creatures first learn about God—and about prayer—from others. Their faith is shaped in large degree by what they have learned from their families and their churches. In our concluding chapter we review the major findings of our study, assessing the importance of a faith community in developing a prayer life and challenging the churches to be instruments in teaching people how to pray.

WORKS CITED

Allport, Gordon W.
  1950   *The Individual and His Religion: A Psychological Interpretation.* New York: Macmillan.
Bellah, Robert N., Richard Madsen, William Sullivan, Ann Swidler, and Stephen Tipton
  1985   *Habits of the Heart: Individualism and Commitment in American Life.* New York: Harper & Row.
Donahue, Michael J.
  1985   Intrinsic and Extrinsic Religiousness: Review and Meta-analysis. *Journal of Personality and Social Psychology* 48:400–419.
Emerging Trends
  1983   How Do Americans Nourish and Strengthen Their Religious Faith? Vol. 5:1–2. Princeton, N.J.: Princeton Religion Research Center.
  1985   Prayer in American Life. Vol. 7:1–2. Princeton, N.J.: Princeton Religion Research Center.
Gallup, George, Jr., and Sarah Jones
  1989   *One Hundred Questions and Answers: Religion in America.* Princeton, N.J.: Princeton Religion Research Center.
Kennedy, Kirk A., and Richard L. Gorsuch
  1989   Gallup Poll on Religion: Social Demographics for Intrinsic and Extrinsic Religious Orientations. Paper presented at the annual meeting of the Society for the Scientific Study of Religion. Salt Lake City, Utah.
Kirkpatrick, Lee A., and Ralph W. Hood, Jr.
  1989   Intrinsic-Extrinsic Religious Orientation: The "Boon" or the "Bane" of Contemporary Psychology of Religion. Paper presented at the meeting of the Society for the Scientific Study of Religion. Salt Lake City, Utah.
Spilka, Bernard, Ralph W. Hood, Jr., and Richard L. Gorsuch
  1985   *The Psychology of Religion: An Empirical Approach.* Englewood Cliffs, N.J.: Prentice-Hall.

7

PRAYER AND COMMUNITY
A Challenge to Churches

> The one difference I see between churchgoers and those with deep spiritual faith is that the latter meet frequently in small groups with others in fellowship, prayer and mutual support. In this setting, people can see the power of prayer and make the exciting discovery that God really cares about them personally.
>
> Michael McManus, religion columnist

Americans are a praying people. This perhaps was never so apparent in recent history as on the eve of the initiation of U.S. military action in the Persian Gulf. Surveys taken at the time showed Americans praying for peace and for God's dominion over events with greatly increased frequency, as well as with new intensity and a sense of urgency. It is not surprising that this should have happened. For most people in this nation prayer is not just a habit or pious duty; it is nothing less than communion with God.

But is prayer effective? Does it make a difference in people's lives? The answer as presented in this book rests not simply with subjective testimonies or with the observations of historians and other social observers, but in a careful examination of the faith lives of the great mass of people as they listen and seek to respond to the voice of God. By means of scientific surveys it is possible in some measure to quantify this response. Before proceeding with a summary and implications of our findings, it is important to note the approach we took to the study. Specifically we want to say a word about the usefulness of statistical analysis, our theoretical perspective, and some of the limitations of our work.

A WORD ABOUT METHODS

Some objection may be raised to using seemingly impersonal survey research to talk about a subject that many regard as very personal and sacred. In no way do we pretend to have the final word on prayer. What we believe our research has done is to add credence to the many devotional and theological writings that exist on the topic. Indeed statistics itself may take on an inspiring quality when one considers the fact that they are not simply a reflection of the prayer lives of a handful of people, or even of the thousand respondents who participated in this survey. Due to the representative nature of Gallup sampling procedures, the persons included in this survey speak for millions of Americans. Although survey research is unable to portray topics with great depth, it does provide an accurate structure into which more intensive writings may be placed.

Some critics have alleged that it is possible to "lie with statistics," distorting the very facts that are being presented. We have not "beat our data into submission," getting it to say what we wanted. Our presentations have been straightforward, although guided by a sympathetic approach to the topic. Specifically, we have rejected a reductionist approach, that is, one that explains away God. It is our conviction that it is fully as intellectually honest to start with the assumption that God is in the picture as to take the opposite position. The reductionist approach has been popular in social science, but it is a perspective that we cannot support. We cannot prove the existence of God through social scientific research, but we can demonstrate some of the effects that God has in the lives of believers. In the words of W. I. Thomas, a leading figure in early American sociology, "If people define situations as real, they are real in their consequences." We believe this stance is more creative, making us more open to discovering the mysteries of prayer and the effects prayer has on those who pray.

Although the Gallup sample is deemed to be representative (see the appendix for details), it cannot be used to answer all of the questions that we may have about prayer in America. It is limited by the sample itself as well as by the number of questions we were able to ask. For example, the vast majority of the sample are self-proclaimed Christians (Protestant, Catholic, or Orthodox). This relative homogeneity, reflecting the Christian dominance in American society, left us with very few Jews, Muslims, Hindus, and members of other non-Christian faiths in each of these subgroups. It was thus impossible for us to demonstrate differences and similiarities between Christian and various non-Christian forms of prayer. This is a topic that must be left to future research.

Nor do we feel that we have exhausted the types of prayer. Undoubtedly further refinements are needed. Our measures of meditative prayer, for example, are rather basic, with fifty percent of the pray-ers having engaged in all four practices (thinking about God, feeling the presence of God, worshiping God, and listening to God) at least on occasion. Spiritual writers tell us there is another form, sometimes referred to as contemplative prayer, which moves the pray-er into a deeper union with God. This too we must leave for further research.

We acknowledge that our approach has some limitations, but we believe it provides a strong base from which to launch other studies on this important and overlooked topic. Our findings demonstrate beyond a reasonable doubt that prayer does make a difference in the lives of Americans.

THE EFFECTIVENESS OF PRAYER

In vast numbers and through a variety of prayer modes, Americans seek to relate to a power outside themselves. The effects are often profound—in terms of life satisfaction, finding purpose and meaning to life, involvement in social and political causes, and the ability to forgive others who have hurt them. Prayer not only comforts; it challenges the pray-er to move toward a greater spiritual maturity.

We discover that a high proportion of the nine in ten people who pray experience a deep sense of peace and the strong presence of God through prayer. Survey respondents also frequently report that they have received an answer to specific prayer requests. Still others say they have gained a deeper insight into some biblical truth, and even that they have been inspired or led by God to perform some specific action. Prayer thus is not just an action on the part of the one who prays; it serves, as the mystics know well, as a means of communing with God who responds to our feeble efforts.

Virtually everyone prays in some fashion, even those who are not connected with faith communities. Of those who pray, the vast majority report that they thank God for his blessings, talk to God in their own words, ask God to forgive their sins, and seek guidance for decisions. For those who converse with God in this manner, their offering of thanks and their requests need not be formal. It may be much like having coffee with a good friend.

But just as coffee companions are not always good listeners, many pray-ers have not learned the art of being still and knowing God is God! Many are more adept at talking than they are at listening for the voice of the Holy One. Our findings show that smaller although still impressive numbers report they have quietly thought about God, have tried to listen to God speaking to them, have spent time worshiping and adoring God, and have felt the strong presence of God in their lives. We have called these people meditative pray-ers who use a meditative prayer form. They are the ones who are most likely to encounter God in prayer.

Broadly speaking, this study reveals that the most profound effects of prayer occur when a person goes beyond rote and ritualistic prayer and senses an intimacy with God. Although the one-sided act of praying may mark the beginning of a person's prayer life, quiet times of waiting and expectation are needed to experience the presence of God. This sense is fostered by religious experiences such as those described in our research—receiving answers to prayer, being inspired to perform specific actions, and feeling the presence of God.

A culture with an emphasis on instant gratification and characterized by a noisy roar and constant bustle does not make meditative prayer easy. Its penchant for fast foods and quick credit does not produce people who are adept at waiting patiently for God's presence to touch them. Modern society's predisposition to fill each moment of silence with sound inhibits passive, quiet forms of prayer which require the pray-er to silence the noise within. In order to pray effectively, we need to step aside from the frantic pace of life and seek solitude. Many may be unwilling or unable to do so.

Yet one of the clear messages to come from this study is the need to listen to God, as well as to speak to God. Elizabeth Emery writes about "the God who cares enough to listen as well as to speak." She observes:

> To be with God involves a relationship in which we are asked to listen as well as to speak. But when do we have time to really listen to anyone? Our lives are controlled by the "tyranny of the urgent." Our days are filled with busi-

> ness noise from dawn to dusk. Even our quiet time has a
> 'doing' quality to it. . . . Are our prayers filled with talking
> to God rather than listening to God? Are we uncomfort-
> able in our corporate worship if there is more than thirty
> seconds of silence?

For those who are able to do as Jesus did—step back from
the hectic demands of daily life to go to the symbolic desert or
mountain—the rewards are great. Such behavior can help bring
about a sense of nearness to God. The nearer one feels to God,
suggest earlier surveys, the better people feel about themselves.
A feeling of closeness to God through the mediation of Jesus
Christ in the case of Christians helps us deal with our sense of
guilt and thus feel better about ourselves and others.

Meditative prayer has special power, and it generates what
has been described as a more mature and healthy form of spirituality. Those who practice meditative prayer are the ones who
are most likely to respond positively to deliberate injury. One of
the most significant findings to emerge from the study is the
verification that prayer plays a vital role in helping people forgive those who have hurt them. This is particularly true of
meditative prayer in which one experiences the strong presence
and grace of God. With this finding we are reminded of St.
Teresa of Avila who asserted that the ulitmate test of the validity of prayer is whether or not this communion with the Divine
enables us to forgive others.

Unless we forgive others, we can be destroyed by
suppressed hate and a sense of injustice being done. It is often
only through forgiveness that we can escape from what appears
to be the cruel capriciousness of life. Prayer—particularly
meditative prayer—is the channel through which God's grace
can flow to help us forgive ourselves and others. It is particularly noteworthy that those who try to follow Jesus' teaching to
"love your enemies and pray for those who persecute you"
(Matt. 5:44) reap the rewards of a more satisfied life.

HOW CAN I LEARN TO PRAY?

When preliminary reports of our research on prayer appeared in some newspapers across the country, we began to receive letters from people asking how they might be able to pray more effectively. It appeared that people were asking questions of themselves: Is prayer changing me? Is it making a difference in my life? Is my prayer life bringing me closer to God? Am I moving toward giving control of my life to God? Do I consistently try to tune into his presence? Are my prayers helping me deal with my own sense of self-worth? Are they helping me develop a more loving relationship with others? Although teaching others to pray effectively is beyond the scope of our work, the questions being asked are worth consideration.

The true measure of prayer is whether it transforms the old self into a new self, and changes the way we relate to others. This is likely to happen not if we limit our attempts to communicate with God to rote prayer offered on the run but rather if we allow ourselves to enter the darkness and silence of our own souls so that light and the voice of God may fill the void. If we allow God the opportunity to come into our private worlds bringing with him the good news of his personal love, we will never be the same. His love will change us.

We are reminded that coming to God need not be a complicated task. We need only recognize that God is near, seeking to lead and empower us. Accept the fact, wrote the late Anglican Bishop Michael Ramsey, that God wants to spend time with us. We are also reminded by the prayer experts that we need not worry so much about what we should say or how we should say it. The starting point is a disposition to prayer, a willingness to have a "heart for God." Start simply, Ramsey suggested, with a prayer such as, "Oh God, teach me to pray." And always bear in mind that God is there to help us in our efforts. Theologian and author Henri Nouwen (1981:73) writes, "God is seeking to guide us, to strengthen us, to purify us, to forgive and save us. When we respond, His presence can become more real to us than anything else in life."

Yet some may be afraid to yield to the divine intimacy God desires to have with each of us in prayer. This fear is not totally unfounded. There are those who believe that God has told them to perform horrible crimes, presumably during some kind of prayer contact. Still others, whose symptoms include hearing the voice of God, have been diagnosed as mentally ill. Can prayer make a person off-balance?

Private prayer, the topic of our research, is by definition a solitary activity. Being social creatures, however, we must learn to pray, and we do so through interaction with other people. Pray-ers have learned to pray at their mother's or father's knee, in praying with friends, by reading books, or through a myriad of other ways. Prayer (just as our other thoughts and actions) is something that has been at least in part learned from others. Continued interaction with other people of prayer can teach the beginner how to move beyond the simplest form of one-way conversational prayer to wordless prayer with deep spiritual encounters. Although far more people pray than belong to a church, we feel it is the church that is in the best position to teach its people more about effective prayer.

OUR CHALLENGE TO THE CHURCHES

The examination of the dimensions and varieties of prayer in American life carried out in our study underscores the need for churches and other faith communities to give new attention to the practical "how to" aspects of our religious lives—how to bring the Bible into one's daily life, how to share one's faith, and how to pray. Clergy and religious educators, we believe it is fair to say, tend to make assumptions about the prayer ability of the laity—to assume that the latter are giving prayer the attention it deserves, are examining various modes of prayer, and are practicing prayer in a consistent way. It is probably far more accurate to say that most Americans, while believing in prayer, are desperately in need of help in understanding and practicing prayer.

If prayer is the wellspring of a life of faith, then churches have their work cut out for them. Many people (and perhaps some church leaders) do not realize that it is not only possible but psychologically beneficial to commune with God. As an aside, not all spiritual encounters have been found to have positive effects. Research done by Margaret Poloma and Brian Pendleton (1991, chap. 5) found that nontheistic psychic and occult experiences were shown to have some negative consequences for psychological well-being, a striking contrast to the positive well-being scores found for those who have prayer experiences. Many people are seeking greater spiritual awareness and may be turning to places other than the churches. These nontheistic experiences not only fail to satisfy the longing of the human heart for God but may actually be harmful to those who seek them.

It is often difficult for a person to develop an active and disciplined prayer life on their own. Clergy and others, therefore, might do well to look into the possibility of starting small groups among parishioners. In such small groups, one can feel the power of prayer in a new way and further strengthen faith. The practice of sharing prayer and the fruits of prayer in small group discussions can do much to help improve private times of prayer.

Preliminary research by the George H. Gallup International Institute reveals that more than one-fourth of Americans are currently meeting in small groups that have a spiritual dimension. The fruits of their experience are remarkable and exciting in terms of deepened faith, prayers being answered, relationships being healed, being better able to forgive themselves and others, and in terms of helping them serve people outside their groups.

Are people ready to take a new look at their prayer lives? The answer would appear to be a convincing Yes. Surveys show that Americans seek to deepen their faith through prayer. They want more help from their churches about how to develop a mature prayer life. Many long for intimacy with God—to experience God. It is to be hoped that the famous social psychologist Abraham Maslow was wrong when he noted nearly thirty years ago that religious institutions seem to be led by "non-peakers" (those who themselves have not had religious experiences) trying to teach other "non-peakers" about "peak experiences." Church leaders need to be men and women of prayer who can direct others along the path of prayer.

RENEWED CHURCHES, RENEWED WORLD

There is much talk in church circles about renewal and evangelism. Any renewal movement of this sort, however, is unlikely to happen if Americans—both churched and unchurched—are not given instruction on prayer and opportunities to deepen their prayer lives. This may come through small groups of various types, through private spiritual direction, or in other ways. A deepened and more meditative style of prayer, we believe, is the starting point for any revitalization of the church in the 1990s.

Fortunately there is a solid basis on which to build renewed prayer lives. Americans believe in the power of prayer and seem eager to bring prayer or communion with God more to the center of their lives. In this respect, it is interesting to note that our prayer attitudes and behavior differ sharply from those of the British public. A 1990 Gallup survey revealed that fully half of British adults—and an even higher percentage of young adults—never pray in any form. Such findings, although they tell us little about the depth and quality of their prayer, will surely worry religionists as they contemplate the future of religion in Great Britain.

Who can begin to calculate the impact deepened prayer lives might have upon our hurting society, hopefully moving the populace to a more peaceful, more forgiving, more positive frame of mind? Lives transformed by prayer can bring about a transformed society. Ultimately our goal is to lead a life of integrated prayer and ministry. Henri Nouwen in *The Way of the Heart* writes, "When we have found our rest in God we can do nothing other than minister."

Over the centuries nowhere has the power of prayer been so dramatically revealed as in the lives of the saints. Prayer was the wellspring of their existence, enabling them to live holy and heroic lives of service. Their lives showed that without sincere prayer one cannot go very far on the road to holiness.

The saints of history shine as guides to how we should strive and live. Also a beacon to those who seek to mature in their faith are the saints of today—the "hidden saints," if you will—who live quietly and selflessly in the lives of others. Although they represent only about one-tenth of the U.S. populace (according to a twelve-item scale developed by the Princeton Religion Research Center), they are having an impact on society far out of proportion to their number. These "modern-day saints," who have a transforming faith, are more charitable toward others, more concerned about the betterment of society, and far happier. A key characteristic of these people is their absolute attention to prayer, making a supreme effort to stay in close communion with God.

But we do not have to be saints—or even saints in the making—to experience the power of prayer. The good news is that prayer—one of God's greatest gifts—is available to all.

WORKS CITED

Emery, Elizabeth
   1990   Are You Listening? *New England Christian* (November).
Nouwen, Henri
   1981   *The Way of the Heart.* New York: Ballantine Books.
Poloma, Margaret, and Brian Pendleton
   1991   *Religiosity and Well-Being: Exploring Neglected Dimen-sions of Quality of Life Research.* Lewiston, N.Y.: Edwin Mellen Press.

METHODOLOGY
APPENDIX
Design of the Samples

FOR PERSONAL SURVEYS

The design of the sample for personal (face-to-face) surveys is that of a replicated area probability sample down to the block level in the case of urban areas and to segments of townships in the case of rural areas.

After stratifying the nation geographically and by size of community according to information derived from the most recent census, over 350 different sampling locations are selected on a mathematically random basis from within cities, towns, and counties that have in turn been selected on a mathematically random basis.

The interviewers are given no leeway in selecting areas in which they are to conduct their interviews. Each interviewer is given a map on which a specific starting point is marked and is instructed to contact households according to a predetermined travel pattern. At each occupied dwelling unit, the interviewer selects respondents by following a systematic procedure. The procedure is repeated until the assigned number of interviews has been completed.

FOR TELEPHONE SURVEYS

The national Gallup telephone samples are based on the area probability sample used for personal surveys.

In each of the sampling locations selected (as described above), a set of telephone exchanges that falls within the geographic boundaries of the sampling location is first identified. Listed telephone numbers in these exchanges are selected randomly and used as "seed numbers" for randomly generating telephone numbers assigned to households within telephone exchanges serving our sampling locations. The final sample of numbers thus reflects the stratification and selection of sampling locations that provide confidence in the representativeness of our area probability sample.

After the survey data have been collected and processed, each respondent is assigned a weight so that the demographic characteristic of the total weighted sample of respondents matches the latest estimates of the demographic characteristics of the appropriate adult population available from the U.S. Census Bureau. Telephone surveys are weighted to match the characteristics of the adult population living in households with access to a telephone. The weighting of personal interview data includes a factor to improve the representation of the kinds of people who are less likely to be found at home.

The procedures described above are designed to produce samples approximating the adult civilian population (18 and older) living in private households (that is, excluding those in prisons, hospitals, hotels, religious and education institutions, and those living on reservations or military bases)—and, in the case of telephone surveys, households with access to a telephone. Survey percentages may be applied to census estimates of the size of these populations to project percentages into numbers of people. The manner in which the sample is drawn also produces a sample that approximates the distribution of private households in the United States; therefore, survey results can also be projected to numbers of households.

INDEX

Adoration, 6, 20, 35
Age universal, 108, 115. *See also*
  Intrinsic religiosity
Akron Area Survey, 13–16, 23,
  33, 53
Allport, Gordon, 108
Answered prayer, 51–52. *See
  also* Petitionary prayer

Bellah, Robert, 68
Benson, Herbert, 10–11
Bloom, Metropolitan Anthony,
  52
Born-again. *See* Evangelicals
Brommer, Josef, 31–32
Burke, Edmund, 67
Byrd, Randolf, 10, 11–12

Catholics, 10, 25, 28, 50, 60
Charismatics, 54–55
Christian Right, the, 69
Church attendance, 14, 64, 104,
  114 n. 2, 121

Colloquial prayer. *See*
  Conversational prayer
Conscience orientation, toward
  religion, 112, 116, 118
Conversational prayer, 15, 20,
  29–31, 36, 40 n. 4, 62, 64, 74,
  99, 117

Daujat, Jean, 19–20
Divine guidance, 45–46, 56–58,
  101
Divine intimacy, 39–40, 44–45,
  61, 64, 100–102, 114 n. 2,
  121–22

Edwards, Denis, 61
Emery, Elizabeth, 128–29
Extrinsic religiosity, 108–9,
  115–16, 119
Evangelicals, 12, 29, 33–34, 50,
  54, 55, 57–58, 59–61, 74,
  75 n. 1

Faith factor, 11
Finney, John R., 7–10
Fitzgibbons, Richard, 87
Forgiveness, 85–88, 111
  attitudes toward, 88–89
  and life satisfaction, 89–94
  NEGACT index, 90–91, 97, 104
  POSACT index, 90–91, 97, 104
  and prayer, 99
  and religiosity, 95–98
  religious orientation, 112–14

Gallup Reports, 1, 3–7, 88, 108, 134
Galton, Francis, 8–9
George H. Gallup International Institute, 133
Glossolalia, 7, 54
Gnostics, 54
Gorsuch, Richard, 108–9, 14
Guideposts, 57

Hope, Donald, 86

Institutional orientations, toward religion, 112, 116, 118
Intercessors, 12
Intercessory prayer. See Petitionary prayer
Intrinsic religiosity, 108–9, 115–16, 119

James, William, 1, 2, 6, 16

Kaufman, Morton, 85
Kierkegaard, Søren, 19, 20

Landor, Walter Savage, 107
Life satisfaction, 13–14, 89, 92–94, 111, 113–15, 118. See also Well-being

McManus, Michael, 125
Mallory, Marilyn, 10
Malony, H. Newton. See Finney, John R.
Maloney, George, 40
Maslow, Abraham, 43–44, 134
Meditative prayer, 6–7, 15, 35–39, 62 n. 4, 64, 74, 80, 99, 104, 114 n. 2, 117–19, 121, 130
Mental health, 9–10, 87
Merton, Thomas, 37
Methodology, 126–28, 137–39
Multiple regression, 40, 60, 62–63, 94, 104, 119

Narcissism, 107
Nouwen, Henri, 135

Parker, William, 9–10
Pattison, E. Mansell, 85
Peace, 46–47
Peak experiences, 43–44
Pendleton, Brian F., 14–15, 133
Petitionary prayer, 8–9, 12, 15, 31–35, 40 n. 4, 51–53, 62 n. 4, 64, 74, 99, 117
Political participation, 76–82, 111, 116–17, 118
Politics, 83–84
  attitudes toward church involvement, 70–76
  and organized religion, 67–70
  and religious salience, 73–74

Prayer
  age differences, 3, 5, 21, 25, 48, 50, 57, 59, 60
  children and, 7–8
  contemplative, 10, 127. See also Meditative prayer
  conversational. See Conversational prayer
  defined, 19
  developmental studies, 7–8
  and forgiveness. See Forgiveness
  frequency of, 2, 3, 14, 21–22, 25
  gender differences, 3, 5, 21, 47, 50, 52, 55, 57, 59, 60, 65 n. 6
  importance of, 5, 107–8
  measurements of, 20–21, 24–39
  meditative. See Meditative prayer
  motivations for, 4–5, 8
  petitionary. See Petitionary prayer
  and politics. See Politics
  and prayer experiences. See Prayer experience
  and relationship with God, 39–40
  and religious maturity, 116–18, 120
  ritual. See Ritual prayer
  verbal. See Verbal prayer
  and well-being, 5, 14
  with others, 23
Prayer experience, 15–16, 46–58, 61–63, 118 n. 3
  and closeness to God, 63–64
  and intrinsic religiosity, 114 n. 2, 115–16
  and politics, 75, 80–81. See also Politics
  and prayer types, 61–63
  scale, 58–59
Privatized religion, 67–68, 76, 110, 114, 116
Protestants, 29, 60
Psychological Abstracts, 86

Ramsey, Michael (Bishop), 131
Relaxation response, 11
Religious belief, 14, 121
Religious experiences, 43–46, 61, 65–66, 82. See also Prayer experiences
Religious motivation and orientation, 109–12
Religious Research Association, 16
Religious salience, 74, 97, 102, 121
Ritual prayer, 15, 24–29, 36, 40 n. 4, 62 n. 4, 64, 117
Rosary, 28

Sacks, Howard, 10
Sagne, Jean-Claude, 31
St. Johns, Elaine. See William Parker
Society for the Scientific Study of Religion, 16
Stark, Rodney, 44–46, 58
Swatos, William, 2

Thanksgiving, 6, 20
Transcendental Meditation, 11

Verbal prayer, 6–7, 9, 37. *See also* Conversational prayer; petitionary prayer; ritual prayer

Well-being, 13–15. *See also* Life satisfaction

Wilson, Woodrow, 107